THE TAN

THE TANGO LESSON
Sally Potter

faber and faber
LONDON · BOSTON

First published in 1997
by Faber and Faber Limited
3 Queen Square London WC1N 3AU

Photoset by Parker Typesetting Service, Leicester
Printed in England by Clays Ltd, St Ives plc

Photographs:
© Adventure Pictures (Tango) Ltd
© Georgui Pinkhassov, Magnum Photos
© Moune Jamet, Sygma
© Richard Kalvar, Magnum Photos
© Martin Weber Sanguinetti, Clarin

A CIP record for this book
is available from the British Library
ISBN 0-571-19166-5

2 4 6 8 10 9 7 5 3 1

CONTENTS

ACKNOWLEDGEMENTS

I am grateful to all the '*tangueros*' of Buenos Aires who warmly welcomed me into their world, taught me how to dance again, and inspired this film.

Walter Donohue kept me on track in his light inimitable fashion whilst I was writing the script (before and during the shoot). Amos Field Reid, my assistant, worked painstakingly behind the scenes. Alexandra Cann, my agent, kept faith and cracked jokes. David Mitchell introduced me to Delacroix's painting of Jacob and the Angel. The Co-producers trusted me, for which I thank them. Christopher Sheppard's dedication and ingenuity made it all possible. Martin Buber wrote *I and Thou* which proved to be a key to understanding the deeper appeal of the dance. And the music of the Argentinian tango, especially the work of Piazzolla and Pugliese, continues to move and amaze me.

The Tango Lesson is dedicated to my beloved father
NORMAN POTTER
1923–1995
in gratitude for all he taught me

and to the memory of
DIEGO FESTA
1979–1996

INTRODUCTION

After I had finished doing the promotion tours for *Orlando* (long after the film was 'finished' for me) I sat down to write. Seven screenplay ideas came tumbling on to the page. I narrowed the field to three. And finally chose to pursue the seventh – an 'entertainment' in Graham Greene's terminology – a thriller set in the fashion industry, called, appropriately, *Rage*. Appropriately, because the subject matter invoked rage in me and proved to be a vehicle for a critical voyage through the vagaries of a glamorous, narcissistic industry founded almost entirely on the exploitation of third world resources and labour. But while I was shaping 'carnage on the catwalk' by day, I was stepping out – for relief and pleasure – to dance by night.

Throughout the *Orlando* years I had been out ballroom dancing two or three times a week – the perfect humble kitsch antidote to the story's highbrow Bloomsbury overtones that I was so keen to avoid. But now I had discovered Argentinian tango – not the stiff, strutting and insipid tango of *Come Dancing*, but the subtle, rapid-fire, close-hold, melancholic, ecstatic dance from Buenos Aires.

My relationship with dance went back a long way. The only formal training I ever had was as a dancer in my early twenties. I never made it to technical perfection because I had started so late. Even at twenty-one I felt too old to become a 'real' dancer. I suffered, physically, in the relentless daily training, but I loved the metaphor it offered as a life lesson. Daily application, practice, attention to detail, a form of disciplined endeavour rooted in the body yet calling to something beyond the physical. And choreography was the perfect 'poor theatre'. All you needed were willing bodies and some space. So it was as a choreographer that I learnt how to direct and it was as a dancer that I learnt how to work. It was in the mute world of the dance that I first discovered, also, the *necessity* to speak.

My choreographies became 'performance art' (an inadequate phrase to describe a form that integrated movement, text and image), and eventually led me back to film – my starting point

vii

when I left school at sixteen to become a film-maker. But in those early days I had lacked the financial resources to produce more than a string of two-minute epics on out of date film stock processed (by me) in the cold and draughty Film Makers Cooperative – mostly abstract visual poems.

So here I was, once again working in film (or trying to); convinced that the world of dance was behind me, except as a private source of knowledge about the struggle to go beyond personal limits, how to organize bodies in space, and, perhaps above all, how to work with music. In the meantime my needs as a performer were being met as a musician – I was touring around Europe in several different improvised music bands, mainly as a singer. My joy was to improvise lyrics and be part of the process of simultaneous group composition.

But once a dancer, always a dancer, they say. I couldn't find a relationship of equanimity with the dance. It was impossible to treat it as a hobby. Every time I started to move it filled me with too much longing. And at the same time, paradoxically, I found it hard to believe I could still take dance so seriously; the most ephemeral of the arts, the easiest to trivialise, the hardest to really 'show'. The conditions had to be so right (good floor, heating, sightlines, etc.) and were usually so wrong. I made some dance films, but discovered that it's even harder to really show what dance is on film. You need to see the whole body, but then you are in danger of losing the energy of the dance and of the medium of film itself by being too formal, too distant.

But by now (1994) I felt I had negotiated, at last, a degree of peace with dance. Post-*Orlando*, having finally 'found my feet' as a film director, it seemed I was able also to enjoy a night out in the dance clubs for pure pleasure, just like anyone else, after doing my *real* work in the day. Or so I thought. And then bit by bit the tango became that which I daydreamed about, puzzled over, longed for (but would definitely *not* make a film about. Oh no).

Meanwhile, the script of *Rage* was finding some favour in the USA. It was time to go and 'take some meetings' over there. I decided to go to Buenos Aires en route to take a closer look at the tango. Just for fun.

And so it began. The schisms in my life – between the world of ideas and the world of the body – between 'serious' work and pure pleasure – between the world of the writer/director and the performer – between doing and being – gradually became the subject matter for a new film.

Meanwhile I was taking tango lessons. I soaked up the teaching in Buenos Aires, hour upon hour, loving being a student again; and then returned to Paris where I had already met Pablo Veron – a young legend within the tango world – to learn some more.

But with him it was more than that. I had seen Pablo on stage at the Folies Bérgère and was fascinated by his combination of technical wizardry and meditative presence. All my director's instincts were stimulated. It was his presence I knew I could work with – a presence much more akin to great film performers than many stage actors. I was falling in love.

But the falling in love was not innocent of intent. Was it love or work? Had I perhaps fallen in work? One night, in a café in Paris, I made a proposal to him: 'If you teach me how to be a tango dancer, a real tango dancer, one day I will put you in a film – I will make you into a star.' We shook hands across the table. And went out dancing.

I abandoned *Rage*, and started work on what was to become *The Tango Lesson*. But what began as a process of integration – of my various lives as dancer, performer, writer, director – became a tightrope walk. The highwire was held taut by the uneasy relationship between reality and fiction. I knew that this story could only be told from the inside out. I knew I had to live it. And despite never having consciously desired to perform on film – being, like many directors, quite camera-shy – I now knew that I *had* to perform in this one because the impetus for the film came out of my own desire to dance. Without the driving force of that longing I would be lost and the film itself would be lost. But I was experienced enough as a screenwriter to know that unless direct experience went through the same disciplined transformation as any other material it would stay in the realm of personal anecdote.

I somehow had to distill what I was living – *use* it – and use myself as raw material from which the film would be shaped. I wanted this film to have the muscular purity of a honed narrative (and life isn't like that) yet with the raw immediacy of lived risk. I wanted it to show, somehow, what dancing *feels* like, rather than what it *looks* like. I wanted to integrate the dance numbers into the story in such a way that the two were indivisible. I wanted to show the 'real' tango, without pretending to come from the inside of the culture that produced it. I wanted to show how at root, social dancing is a philosophical enquiry into the nature of the eternal other – without words, but with all the accuracy of intent. I wanted to ask lots of questions about love and work and creation. About how inventing (as Martin Buber says) seems really to be a question of finding. And how film-making (and writing) seems to really be about looking (and listening). And in the meantime I was listening to hundreds of tangos – discovering the extraordinary compositional wealth of a music rarely heard outside Argentina.

In other words, what had started out as entertainment on the sidelines of my life had *become* my life. And my life was, as usual, defined by work. And work was love.

How to describe the film? A musical? (How wonderful to try and re-invent a form that seemed to have got stuck in the forties.) And the characters? What about names? Eventually, with some trepidation, I decided to use my own and Pablo's real names, as a sort of 'double cover'. With invented names I felt it would seem that I was trying to hide something. With our own – given how the film would be as tightly written and structured as any fiction – I could work directly with the notion of exposure, vulnerability, seeing and being seen. The story itself would become a sort of unravelling of truths about identity.

Identity itself, of course, is also bound up with language. I am English, Pablo is Argentinian, but our common language is French. The issue of what language to make the film in became an interesting conundrum, and seemed, somehow, symptomatic of deeper issues in the story. We were both outsiders (me in Argentina, Pablo in Europe) and each laboured under the constant necessity to find a translation for terms and experiences unfamiliar to the other. The world of cinema was new to Pablo and the world of professional tango dancing was new to me. A large part of my work as a screenwriter and director was to find a way of translating, literally and metaphorically, one language into another – the language of dance into the language of film. At that point Pablo spoke very little English at all.

On top of that, the issue of domination of the world cinema market by the English language and the struggle of other nations (especially the French) to maintain their own language on screen,

meant that any choice could not be innocent of political implication.

Eventually, I decided to shoot the scenes between Pablo and myself in both French *and* English, and the scenes in Buenos Aires in English and Spanish depending on what was natural for the characters. In effect, the film would have to move fluidly between languages as we did in real life, and had to become emblematic of the nature of cultural exchange. In the process I became fascinated by what was, essentially, untranslatable and even unsayable. I had to identify what can *only* be said in words, what can only be spoken in movement, and what can only be articulated by music.

So, bit by bit, the key decisions were made. The film would be shot in three languages, in three countries and I would occupy three roles – as writer, director and performer. It was only during the shoot itself that I woke up to the consequences of the decisions I had taken. As a performer I lacked a director, and often felt very alone. And as a director I lacked my eyes, because I was in front of the camera. I had to relinquish some of the controls I thought were essential to directing. I had to learn to work with the essential drive of the story from the inside looking out, rather than from the outside looking in. And I had to learn to do it all on a fraction of the sleep I really needed, with aching muscles and sometimes, literally, bleeding feet.

But the joy was, and is, as always, in creating a context for *learning*. And the process of making the film became a sequence of unforgettable lessons, albeit learned under conditions of extremity.

The more that I danced the more lessons I learned: that this most physically active and demanding of the arts is essentially about stillness. That music is, at its core, a way of describing silence. That performing is more about the invisible inside than the visible outside. (Never attempt to 'show' something.) That Martin Buber and the early Jewish mystics have more to say about the nature of the tango than any modern dance critic (see *I and Thou*). That pleasure – taken to its extremity – becomes work. And work – taken to its extremity – becomes love. So, I started out trying to make a film about dance and ended up making a story about love.

Sally Potter, 1997

The Tango Lesson

FRONT CREDITS SEQUENCE

A round white table.
A hand appears and wipes the table, back and forth, until it is
gleaming, white.

SP sits at the table and arranges a stack of clean white sheets of paper in
front of her.
The white table, white paper.
White sunlight through a window.
She sits immobile. Concentrated, waiting.

The sounds of breath, and thought. Low threshold sounds like the pulse
of electricity, or of the sea in the distance.
And then she lifts a pencil, slowly.
The pencil point hovers over the page.

A woman in red, running, running, by a green hedge; her
long red hair and long red dress streaming out behind her.

And then SP's hand is writing, fast, the word RAGE.

A gunshot.
The woman falls to the ground in a billowing cloud of red
silk.

SP screws up the piece of paper she was writing on and tosses it to the
floor.

FRONT CREDITS CONTINUE

The fashion designer, a man without legs, his short hair
dyed blond, sits in a wheelchair, watching intently as three
young women, models, teetering in immensely high heels,
slowly mount a stone staircase.

Long black hair with a yellow dress.
Long fair hair with a blue dress.

3

And the woman with long red hair and a red dress.
The backviews of the three women; statuesque, excessively
slender, their long, long hair trailing down their backs,
their long, long dresses trailing behind them as a
photographer darts around them, snapping.
Flash, flash.

SP sits and writes at the white table. Fast. Intense.

FRONT CREDITS COME TO AN END

STREET/EXT. THEATRE – NIGHT

SP walking along a Paris street. Bright twinkly lights. Traffic. Noise.
And then softly, seductively, the vivid, melancholic strains of a tango
seep out from the doors of a theatre as she passes.
She stops, hesitates, turns, and then follows the sounds into the lobby of
the theatre.

LOBBY AND AUDITORIUM OF THEATRE – NIGHT

SP crosses the lobby under the chandeliers towards the music. She enters
the back of a crowded auditorium and squeezes along past the back row
of the audience until she can see the stage.
Bright, bright spotlights on a dark stage.

A couple – dark, sinuous and concentrated – are dancing the
Argentinian tango in the spotlight. Intimate, dramatic, and very fast.
SP stands at the back of the auditorium in the shadows, watching,
curious at first and then increasingly mesmerized by the dancing and by
the music (Quejas de Bandoneon).

At the end of the number, the audience bursts into applause.
The couple take their bows.
The man – Pablo – reaches out to the audience, arms outstretched, but
relaxed. Self-contained.
He bows, but his eyes never leave the auditorium.
His public.
Love me, he says with his smile. I will let you love me.

SP watches and she sees.

THEATRE BAR (PARIS) – NIGHT

SP sitting at a table, in a corner of the bar, surveying the scene.

Pablo appears with his dance partner. They are surrounded by friends and admirers. SP gets up and crosses the lobby towards them where they stand by the shiny counter in front of the rows of glittering glasses and bottles.

                              SP
   Señor Veron?

Pablo turns towards her, politely.

                              PABLO
  Si?

                              SP
Do you speak English?

                              PABLO
A little . . .
                              (*Spanish*)
Do you speak Spanish?

5

SP
(Spanish)

Very little.

PABLO
(French)

Well, we're in Paris, so let's speak in French.

SP hesitates.

SP
(French)

I wanted to say . . . I think you move like an angel.

Pablo bows his head politely.

PABLO
(French)

Thank you very much.

SP
(French)

But it's more than that. You give, but not too much. In fact, you use your presence on stage like an actor on film.

Pablo's expression shifts, almost imperceptibly. He looks at her quizzically, for a moment.

PABLO
(casually)

Do you work in the cinema?

SP

Yes.

Pablo smiles. And moves a little closer. SP hesitates, momentarily, smiling at him and then . . .

Do you give tango lessons?

Pablo's partner's eyes flicker towards them. She looks SP up and down.

PABLO

Yes. Yes.

6

The lights in the bar are twinkling, glittering and glowing around them like fireflies.

PARK (PARIS) – DAY

SP standing at the top of a wide flight of steps. Stone steps in a formal French park.

She takes a photograph with a tiny camera and then runs down the stairs and sits among the metallic chairs grouped haphazardly at the bottom.
SP sits very still and stares at the stone staircase.

The three young women in their long, long dresses turn slowly to face SP.
Red, yellow, blue.

SP frowns, concentrated, staring at the space ahead and into the space inside her head.

SP walking past a long low hedge. Crouching.
Tracking like a camera.
And then running, fast.

SP walking by a low stone wall by a small lake in the park.
And then bending down to peer between the balustrades towards the fountains.
Hand over hand; her hands walking along the parapet. She stands and stares intently out over the water.

PABLO'S APARTMENT (PARIS) – DAY

SP climbs the stairs in an old French building.

INTERTITLE: THE FIRST LESSON

She presses a doorbell and waits.
The door creaks open and Pablo appears, crumpled and unshaven, in a tracksuit and dressing-gown, his face full of sleep.

SP
(*hesitantly*)

Hello.

PABLO
(*surprised*)

Hello.

He looks blank. Sniffs. And then realizes.

It's today?

SP

I think so. Yes.

Pablo strikes his forehead in mock horror and then opens the door wide.

PABLO
(*French*)

Come in . . .

An enormous, empty room. Empty apart from piles of builders' rubble, heaps of cardboard boxes, a bicycle.

Pablo momentarily disappears into the kitchen and then returns, drinking some maté tea.

PABLO

Do you dance?

SP

Well, not really. But I'm ready to begin.

Pablo puts down his maté, and takes off SP's coat.

PABLO

Okay.

He throws her coat onto a pile of rubble.

There's no music.

He takes her hands and places them in position – her right hand in his, her left hand on his shoulder.

PABLO
(*French*)

We walk.

He starts to lead her.
He walks forward. She walks backward.

8

Walk, just walk.
Fluid. Normal.

SP is looking down at her feet.

> SP
> (*French*)
> (*laughing shyly*)
> You know, it's really difficult to walk backwards.

> PABLO
> (*French*)
> Okay. So let's walk forwards. Off we go . . . One . . . two . . .
> three . . .

They walk forwards. SP stumbles and then stops.

> SP
> (*French*)
> (*laughing*)
> And now I feel I can't walk at all.

*Pablo looks SP up and down as she stands, immobile in front of him;
then takes off her jacket, decisively.*

> PABLO
> (*French*)
> Okay. Just find your centre.

*SP sways. Pablo leaps forward and adjusts her axis. She looks down.
He lifts her chin. He touches her back, her shoulders, her stomach.
She turns her head slowly and looks at him.*

EXT. STREET AND WHITE ROOM (LONDON) AND PARK (PARIS) –
DAY

*SP crosses the road carrying her suitcase and climbs the clanking metal
fire escape of an industrial building. Home.*

SP sitting at the round white table.
She sharpens a pencil decisively.

**High heels teetering dangerously, on the stone steps. Ankles
wobbling.**

9

*It's the young woman in yellow with long black hair. She
stumbles, her high-heeled shoe catching in the train of her
dress.
Down, down, down, she falls.
Down the stone staircase.
Onto her head.*

*The woman in blue and the woman in red scream
soundlessly.*

*A horrible silence.
The slow trickle of blood.*

SP sitting motionless at the white table. Frozen.

*The woman in yellow lying on the cold steps. Her dead eye
glazed, open.
The photographer adjusting her hair as he clicks,
feverishly.
Flash. Flash.*

SP slowly puts down her pencil. Gets up. Goes to the window. Stands
and stares into the distance.

*The woman with long fair hair dressed in blue and the
woman with long red hair dressed in red are lowering
themselves into a small rowing boat, accompanied by three
seamstresses dressed in black. The fashion designer wheels
himself along beside the stone wall by the lake, stops,
turns, and peers out between the balustrades as the little
boat is pushed out into the water.*

SP is now at the table again, writing furiously.

*The woman in blue and the woman in red are perched,
perilously, on floating shells on the lake.*

*The fashion designer hauls himself out of his wheelchair
onto the low stone wall. He walks, hand over hand,
gracefully, and then gestures for the women to turn. Turn
around, says his hand.*

*They turn, wobbling horribly, as the shells float between
the fountains.*

But a crowd of paparazzi are calling from above – flashing and clicking furiously. The blonde turns and waves.
She wobbles.
A gunshot.
She falls.

She falls into the dark, wintry water of the pond, her hair fanning out above her head like fronds of waving yellow weed.

SP sits motionless at the table.
Puts down her pencil.
Sighs.

And then slowly gets up from the table and starts pacing back and forth.
The pacing turns into walking. Walking backwards.
She looks down at her feet.
And slowly, with a little smile, raises a hand and lifts her chin.

CHURCH HALL (LONDON) – DAY

SP opens the door into a small, bleak English church hall. The hall is festooned with tawdry decorations and balloons and the walls are lined with child-size chairs.

INTERTITLE: THE SECOND LESSON

SP passes a trestle table of teas and biscuits, takes off her coat, and sits down on a tiny chair.

Some couples are creeping – politely but passionately – around the floor to a kitsch rendition of a tango (La Cumparsita).
English faces sitting watching, stiffly, as they sip their tea. SP is a wallflower, watching it all.

And then a short, fat man asks her to dance. They shuffle around on the spot together. He smiles at her, nervously. She smiles politely back at him. The clink of teaspoons as the music comes to an end.

WHITE ROOM (LONDON) AND PARK (PARIS) – DAY

SP is stacking and arranging the papers on her table decisively.
Order. A fresh start.

The woman dressed in red is walking, slowly and gingerly, along the long formal path by the green hedge. She is supported on either side by two men who look like bodyguards. They are wearing dark suits and dark glasses. But they are moving rather strangely.

They are moving strangely because these men are wearing black ballet shoes beneath their black suits.. Staggering, painfully, on point along the gravel path.

The fashion designer is wheeling himself backwards, looking intensely at the trio as the photographer darts around them, clicking and flashing.

SP picks up her pencil and is about to write when she sees a tiny spot on the white table. She rubs at it. Rubs and rubs.

Two bowls of water. The men's feet are being lowered trembling into the bowls. Little curls of blood are snaking away from their bleeding toes into the water.

SP fetches a cloth and rubs harder at the invisible mark on the white surface of the table.

The woman in red bends over and looks into the bowls of water. Looks at the bleeding feet. And then kicks off her high heels and starts to run – fast – beside the green hedge; her long red dress snaking out behind her.

The fashion designer is in pursuit in his wheelchair blowing a whistle clamped between his teeth.

Paparazzi are running on the other side of the hedge, calling and clicking. Flash, flash, flash.

SP sits motionless, pencil in hand, as the crunching sound of wheels turning on gravel and the piercing shrieks of the fashion designer's whistle fill the white room.

And then the gunshot. Bang.
The woman with red hair falls to the ground in a billowing cloud of red silk.

SP sighs. Slowly stands. And then starts walking around and around on the white floor. Pacing backwards and forwards. And then just backwards. Practising her basic tango steps.
But something stops her.
She looks down at the floor.
And then kneels down to examine something more closely.

WHITE ROOM (LONDON) – DAY

    INTERTITLE: THE THIRD LESSON

                        BUILDER
                        (voice off)
Immaculate, isn't it?

The builder is walking around the white room, peering into the corners. SP kneels on the floor.

                        SP
Well . . . it's this crack.

The builder walks over and looks down at SP who is staring, fixedly, at an imperceptible crack between the boards.

> BUILDER
> Teaspoon of Polyfilla'd sort that out, wouldn't it?

SP sits back on her heels and looks at him.

> SP
> *(disappointed)*
> Really? . . .

The builder looks at her, looks at the floor.

Then, with a practised, agile, and violent gesture he wrenches the offending floorboard up.
SP peers into the gaping hole in the floor and then looks at the builder.

> SP
> Bad?

> BUILDER
> *(heavily)*
> Bad . . .

He sighs, shakes his head.
SP smiles, faintly, as he casts his eyes over the rest of the floor. He looks knowing. He's seen it all before.

> *(innocently)*
> . . . anywhere you could go for a couple of weeks?

SP tries to hide her pleasure.

TAXI (BUENOS AIRES) – DAY

Heat blasting in through the open windows of a taxi as it weaves perilously in and out of the traffic.
Horns blaring, trucks shinily lurching.
Pollution, dust, noise.

This is Buenos Aires.

A little fan attached to the dashboard, whirring rhythmically.

And FM Tango blasting tinnily from the car radio: Carlos Gardel singing (Mi Buenos Aires Querido).

SP stares happily out of the windows.

CAFE (BUENOS AIRES) – DAY

A huge, cavernous, cool, shadowy art nouveau room, filled with dark wooden tables and chairs and a sea of white table-cloths.

A row of bored elderly waiters in white jackets are standing silently in the distance leaning on a counter as Gardel's voice echoes through the room.

One other customer is sitting reading a newspaper and drinking a small coffee.

SP sits down at a table, takes off her sunglasses, and tries to attract the attention of the waiters.

After an eternity a waiter slowly approaches.

> WAITER
> (*Spanish*)

Good morning.

                              SP
                          (*Spanish*)
                          (*politely*)
          Good morning. A coffee and a . . .

She mimes a crescent shape.

                          WAITER
                          (*Spanish*)
          A croissant?

                              SP
                          (*Spanish*)
          Yes.

                          WAITER
                          (*Spanish*)
          Very well.

*SP looks around her and sighs contentedly as Gardel's song draws to a
close.*

GUSTAVO'S STUDIO (BUENOS AIRES) – DAY

A small dance studio – shabby, mirrored, cool.

*Gustavo smiles, welcomingly, as he stands in the entrance to a small
sunny kitchen holding a kettle.*
Fabian sits on a stool by a piano, watching.

                          GUSTAVO
          Have you danced tango before?

                              SP
          I've had one lesson. In Paris.

                          GUSTAVO
          With?

                              SP
          Pablo Veron.

Gustavo turns and exchanges a knowing glance with Fabian.

GUSTAVO

Ah.

And then Gustavo is teaching SP, leading her gently through the basic tango moves.

GUSTAVO

Now . . . turn.
When you open you have to be in front of the man. Always like this.

He gestures, indicating a man and woman, feet squarely planted as they face each other.
And then 'ochos' (figures of eight); 'giros' (turns): the basic language of rotation. The hips, the feet. Turning, circling.
SP is staring at her feet.
Gustavo lifts her chin and smiles, gently.
She smiles, gratefully, in return.

Now . . . Stay here . . .

He pushes her foot along the ground in an elegant sweep. She laughs delightedly.

Good. Right . . .
Do you know the 'boleo'?

SHOE SHOP (BUENOS AIRES) – DAY

SP is sitting on a chair in a dance shoe shop surrounded by opened boxes of twinkly high heeled shoes.

Her street shoes – rather mannish, sensible boots – sit to one side as she tries on a pair of spindly white high heels.

The shoe man kneels attentively at her feet.

SHOE MAN
(*Spanish*)

Yes?

SP hesitates, polite but doubtful.

(*Spanish*)
Er . . . any in black?

SHOE MAN
(*Spanish*)
(*smiling enthusiastically*)
Black? Yes, I have black as well . . . Yes. Another nice model.
Very nice. Just a minute, I'll be right back with them.

And then SP is teetering along an echoing marble corridor in the shop in
spindly black high heels.
Clearly, it's a new experience.
She steps into a sunbeam and a tango begins (Rawson) . . .

GUSTAVO'S STUDIO (BUENOS AIRES) – DAY

. . . and continues, as SP's black high-heeled foot sweeps along the floor
and kicks between Gustavo's legs.
Gustavo is teaching SP 'ganchos'.

GUSTAVO
Stronger . . .

SP kicks particularly violently.

Well – not *so* strong.

Gustavo and SP laugh.

Higher . . .
Very good.

And then SP is handed back and forth between Gustavo and Fabian.
They cover their balls, like footballers, to protect themselves from the
lethal kicking high-heeled shoes.
Laughing and falling about in their jeans and trainers.
Playing like big puppies as they teach.

They encourage SP.
She is glowing.
Nourished, held, in the private world of the lesson.

DANCE HALL (BUENOS AIRES) – NIGHT

And then they are in the public world of the 'milonga', the dance hall.
Fat people, thin people, old people, young people, beautiful people,
grotesque people. All dressed up for a night out.
SP is sitting at a table with Gustavo, Fabian and Olga.

And then an older man, short, fat, crosses the hall. He bows and asks
Gustavo's permission to dance with SP.

SP rises from her seat, and follows him out onto the floor. Towering
above him.
He is round and he moves round and round like a magical car through
the traffic of the dance floor to the echoing music (El Flete).

And then, SP is dancing with Gustavo.
Then dancing with Fabian, while Gustavo dances with his large,
magnificent wife, Olga.

SP gradually becomes more at ease, hypnotized by the music and the
dancing, as she dances, again and again, with different men.

And then Carlos approaches SP – dark flashing eyes, a brooding almost
violent presence. He holds SP in his arms as if she is a precious jewel.
Possessive. Tight. She closes her eyes, loses herself to the dance.
The music ends. Carlos takes SP back to her seat and mutters rapidly to
Gustavo.

CARLOS
(*Spanish*)

It was a pleasure. She's a good dancer.

HOTEL LOBBY (BUENOS AIRES) – DAY

SP enters a hotel lobby in the early hours of the morning. A sleepy porter
greets her from behind a desk, looking pointedly at his watch and
shaking his head.

PORTER
(*Spanish*)

Good morning.

19

                              SP
                          (*Spanish*)
Good morning.

The porter hands a pile of faxes to SP with her room key.

                          PORTER
                    (*muttering in Spanish*)
         Lots of faxes, eh? Lots of faxes.

                              SP
                          (*Spanish*)
Thank you.

She looks at the faxes blankly.
Flicks through the curling pages, and sighs.

HOTEL ROOM AND BATHROOM (BUENOS AIRES) – DAY

SP closes the shutters in the hotel room against the sun and traffic noise.
Runs a bath.
Then sits on the edge of the bath and eases her aching feet into the water.
She lifts the phone and starts to dial.

                          PRODUCER
         Hello there. Did you get my fax?

                              SP
Yes, I just got in.

                          PRODUCER
         So – they like the idea.

                              SP
They *do*? They like it?

                          PRODUCER
         Yes. But . . .

                              SP
But they want to see a script.

                          PRODUCER
         Right.

                              20

SP sighs.

SP

When do they want it?

SP lying in bed, staring sleeplessly, exhausted, into the darkness; the sounds of morning activity in the street outside.

STREET AND WHITE ROOM (LONDON) – DAY

SP slams the door of the taxi. Crosses the road. And heaves her suitcase up the metal fire escape.
Inside, she drops her suitcase.
And stands and stares.
The once immaculate white room now has no floor.
Exposed joists, builders' rubble, furniture and boxes in heaps.
Destruction and chaos.

WHITE ROOM (LONDON) – NIGHT

SP roughly cleaning the messy, chaotic white table.
Blowing the dust from her script.
The table is perched on some boxes in isolated splendour in the middle of the half-destroyed room.

SP turns the pages of the script, decisively editing and scribbling notes as she goes.

WHITE ROOM (LONDON) AND PARK (PARIS) – DAY

The woman in red lies prone, face down, by the green hedge. Apparently dead.
The fashion designer swings down out of his wheelchair on his strong arms, and reaches out gently to turn her over.
But as she turns, she reaches into the bodice of her dress and pulls out a gun.

And then –

A drop of water falls onto the page.
SP hesitates.
Another drop.
She slowly raises her eyes to the ceiling.

21

Bang, crash, bang.
The sounds of a building site.
A building being demolished.
SP turns to the builder who is noisily stacking floorboards behind her as
she writes.

SP

Excuse me. Excuse me . . .

She gestures at her script.

Water.

The builder staggers across the gaping floor towards SP. They stand
together looking up at the ceiling.
At the drops of water falling, rhythmically, from the leaking roof.

SP

Bad?

She looks at the builder. He grimaces.

BUILDER

Bad.

And now, it seems, the woman dressed in red is chasing
the fashion designer.
He looks back over his shoulder as he runs away from her,
fast, on his hands.
She is bearing down on him, her red dress and red hair
streaming out behind her in the wind as she points the gun
wildly around her, first at the fashion designer and then at
the paparazzi leaping up and down on the other side of the
hedge.

And then there is a gunshot.
Bang. She falls.

Crash!
SP throws down her pencil in shock as rubble cascades onto her script.
She looks up.
Part of the ceiling has caved in.
The builder's face appears, innocently, through the hole in the roof.

PABLO'S APARTMENT (PARIS) – DAY

INTERTITLE: THE FOURTH LESSON

The staircase.
The door bell.
Pablo opens the door.

SP
(*smiling*)

Bonjour.

They look at each other. An open, friendly look.

PABLO
(*French*)

Hi! Come in . . .

Pablo ushers SP into his apartment which now looks clean, ordered and elegant.

It's been a long time.

SP
(*politely*)

Yes. It has.

He takes off her jacket and lays it neatly on the arm of a sofa.

PABLO

Ready?

SP

Yes.

He takes her hands and puts them into the basic tango hold. She smiles.

PABLO

We walk.

She nods, assentingly.
He starts to lead her, in silence.
Delicate, small backwards steps. Walks. Swivels. Turns. Gradually becoming more and more complicated.
She follows well.

Pablo stops and scrutinizes her lightly.

> PABLO
>
> Tell me, have you been dancing a lot?

SP smiles, shyly.
Pablo shifts gear.
He takes a remote control device from his pocket and presses a button.
Music. An austere but increasingly passionate tango (Zum).
And then he gently takes her in his arms, and they start to dance, really
dance, for the first time.

DANCE SALON (PARIS) – NIGHT

The same music continues but now they are dressed for a night out,
dancing in a deserted Parisian dance salon. The waiters are packing up
the tables and chairs around them.

One or two stragglers sit and watch, bemused, as Pablo and SP
continue to dance together – on and on.
Eventually the room is empty: bare, stark, and shadowy. But Pablo
and SP are still dancing.
In a world of their own.

THE SEINE (PARIS) – NIGHT

SP and Pablo are walking through the cold night air, next to the
flowing dark water of the Seine.

> SP
>
> How did you choose the tango?

> PABLO
>
> I didn't choose the tango.
> The tango chose me.

SP laughs as they continue to stroll.

> SP
> (*studiedly casual*)
> And how is your dance partner?

PABLO

We have separated.

He pauses. The silence expands.

In principle.

SP looks at his face as he looks away into the water. A huge bateau-mouche rumbles and growls past them, throwing a violent white light over their faces and bodies. The commentary on board is followed by the tinny, amplified sound of a tango waltz.

And then Pablo turns towards SP again.

PABLO

Have you finished your script?

SP

More or less.

PABLO
(*French*)

Fabulous!

SP shrugs, smiling.

SP

Perhaps.

Pablo leaps down a little flight of steps and breaks into a tap phrase – a brief pastiche of the dance vocabulary of the musicals of the forties.

SP laughs appreciatively.

PABLO
(*casually*)

You know – I always wanted to be in films.

SP smiles and gently puts her hand on his shoulder. They start to dance. Pablo twirls her about under the arch of the bridge to the distorted sound of the waltz from the bateau-mouche as it casts its vivid light over the banks of the Seine.

SP
(*breathless, smiling*)

You know, *I* always wanted to be a dancer.

The sound of the waltz (Amor y Celos) grows and fills the night air as Pablo and SP continue dancing.

The bare wintry trees beside the river are festooned with twinkling lightbulbs, reflected in the water. Christmas is coming.

It's a fast, joyful, celebratory dance under the lights in the frosty air by the dark water.
Snowflakes drift down around them as they dance and twirl about, intoxicated with cold and pleasure, generating their own heat.

CAFE (PARIS) – NIGHT

    INTERTITLE: THE FIFTH LESSON

SP and Pablo are sitting opposite each other at a table in a small Parisian café.

PABLO
(*French*)

Do you think that people's paths cross for a reason?

SP
(*French*)
It depends if you believe in chance or destiny.

PABLO
(*French*)
And you? What do *you* believe?

SP
(*French*)
I believe chance gives us the opportunity to *create* destiny.

PABLO
(*French*)
How?

SP
(*French*)
(*lightly*)
With our will.

PABLO
(*French*)
A question . . . Do you believe in God?

SP
(*laughing*)
Just a little question, eh? Hmm . . .
I don't believe our lives are already written. I don't believe
there is a superior power controlling what we do. Therefore, I
suppose I'm an atheist. But . . .

She pauses and looks away briefly.

. . . but I *feel* I'm a Jew. And you?

PABLO
I am a dancer.

She smiles as he hesitates, searching her face.

And a Jew.

Then they fall into silence.
SP takes Pablo's hand and they look into each other's eyes.

29

A landscape of subtle shifts of expression as each opens to the other. The eyes like pools, becoming transparent.

The eyes slowly filling with water.
Pools of water.
Pools that overflow, delicately.
A tear runs simultaneously down each of their cheeks.

ROISSY AIRPORT (PARIS) – DAY

SP and Pablo skipping up an escalator in the huge white modern railway station at the airport.
Loading SP's suitcase onto a trolley on the shiny white marble floor.

And then they are on parallel tracks on a moving walkway. Pablo on one track, SP on the other, going in opposite directions. They mime a sequence of goodbyes, leaving and returning, close and far, far and close. It's light, it's happy.
Then Pablo leaps across the barrier between the tracks and stretches out across the travelator, blocking SP's path.
She leans over and kisses him, sensuously.

> PABLO

Sally . . .

And then he jumps up and slides along the barrier out of sight.
But as SP approaches the end of the travelator he leaps back into view again, grinning.

> PABLO
> (*French*)

Good luck in Hollywood!

And then they really are going in different directions. SP turns back to wave at the tiny spinning figure in the distance.
Goodbye. A sweet, sweet goodbye.

HOTEL ROOM (LOS ANGELES) – NIGHT

SP lies awake, staring into the darkness.
The small muted electronic sounds of a modern hotel fill the stillness: the soft whine of an elevator shaft; the hum of air conditioning.

SP switches on the light, picks up her book, and starts to read.
The cover of the book shows the bearded Jewish philosopher Martin
Buber. The title: I and Thou.

PABLO'S BATHROOM (PARIS) – DAY

Pablo is lying in his bath – propping up a book in front of him on a
soap rack.
On the cover of the book is a dramatic black and white portrait of
Marlon Brando: it is his autobiography.

Pablo lowers the book and stares at himself in the mirror.

HOTEL ROOM (LOS ANGELES) – NIGHT

SP slowly lowers I and Thou *and stares dreamily in the distance. She*
sighs, happily.

SWIMMING POOL (LOS ANGELES) – DAY

THE SIXTH LESSON

Sunshine glitters on the still water of a swimming pool in Los Angeles.
Three movie executives sit side by side in the shade, opposite SP, who
sits facing them in the full glare of the sun.

The intelligent-looking blonde female movie executive is holding a script
in front of her. The title, written in large black letters, is Rage.

> FEMALE EXECUTIVE
> It's great.
> We love the costumes, and we love the colours.

> 1ST MALE EXECUTIVE
> We love the murders.

> 2ND MALE EXECUTIVE
> Or *are* they murders?

> 1ST MALE EXECUTIVE
> But we want to hear it from *you*, Sally.

> SP
> It's about beauty. And the glamorization of death.

2ND MALE EXECUTIVE
(*smiling*)
It's clear what it's *about*.

1ST MALE EXECUTIVE
But what's the *pitch?* What's gonna make us write you a
cheque for 20 million?

*SP scans their smiling faces. Their white, even teeth. She takes a
breath.*

SP
(*quietly*)
It's set in Paris. A French fashion designer starts to resent the
amount of media attention paid to his models. But then, one
by one, his models mysteriously die . . .

2ND MALE EXECUTIVE
(*interrupting*)
Sally, could you speak up a bit? I can't hear you.

SP
One by one, mysteriously, the models die, which, of course,
only increases the media frenzy. Finally, the only one left is
his favourite, his muse. And then . . .

*SP opens her palms and gestures towards them as if inviting them to
draw their own conclusions.*

1ST MALE EXECUTIVE
Carnage on the catwalk. I love it . . .

SP sits very still, hearing her own words, as if for the first time. Frozen.

2ND MALE EXECUTIVE
So, who is the murderer? Who done it?

1ST MALE EXECUTIVE
Do you even know? The ending seems kinda vague.

FEMALE EXECUTIVE
(*teasingly*)
The writer should know everything. The writer is God, Sally.

Silence in the hot sun.

And then a starlet screams with pleasure, piercingly, as a man standing in the pool smoking a cigar splashes water over her.
SP, startled, turns to look.

> 1ST MALE EXECUTIVE
>
> It says here that the designer has no legs. Why?

> SP
>
> Why not?

> 1ST MALE EXECUTIVE
>
> Casting problems, Sally. You are limiting the market right there.

SP winces.

> FEMALE EXECUTIVE
>
> And it says here – 'They speak in French'. Why?

> SP
>
> They *are* French.

> 1ST MALE EXECUTIVE
>
> If it's not in English we'll lose 75 per cent of the market. Minimum.

> FEMALE EXECUTIVE
>
> Couldn't the story be set somewhere else?

> 2ND MALE EXECUTIVE
> (*quietly*)
>
> Like . . . New York?

SP stares wordlessly at the executives as the sound of a roaring tidal wave builds to a crescendo.

PABLO'S APARTMENT (PARIS) – NIGHT

SP strikes a match.
She stands by a table laid for dinner for two, lighting the candles on a menorah.

> SP
> (*French*)
>
> I've decided to abandon my film.

34

Pablo is standing in the doorway to his kitchen, looking at her, shocked.

> PABLO
> (*French*)
>
> Really? Why?

> SP
> (*French*)
>
> I don't like the script.

> PABLO
> (*French*)
>
> But it was your idea, wasn't it?

> SP
> (*French*)
>
> Yes . . . but I ended up writing a film I wouldn't want to make.

> PABLO
> (*French*)
>
> So what are you going to do?

> SP
> (*French*)
>
> I don't know . . . something more personal.

She lights the last candle, leans against the table and slowly turns to look at Pablo.

> Maybe something to do with the tango.

They exchange a look of playful complicity.

Pablo twirls a dishcloth in his hands.

And then he is in the kitchen, taking lettuce leaves out of the sink and brushing them on the wall, like a drummer brushing a drum. Soft, rhythmic taps.
Taps which form the soft base for a rhythm that builds and builds as he turns every action in the kitchen into a sound, a movement, an improvised choreography – a 'danse de cuisine'.

SP watches him quietly, tenderly.
And then she sits at the table, her face soft and concentrated.

She looks at him with the eyes that, not so long ago, had stared at a flight of steps in a cold French park. The eyes of a camera.
The more Pablo feels her gaze, the more inventive he becomes.

Pablo smiles at SP. Runs to her and spins her around, then leaps up on the mantelpiece, and starts to tap; dancing with his reflection in the mirror.
He looks down at her staring face, at the love and appreciation in her eyes. The rhythm builds to a climax. He stops and pauses for a moment – a tiny moment. Then folds his arms and speaks.

> PABLO
>
> Sally; I have an invitation to dance in Paris in a show . . .

> SP
>
> Oh yes?

> PABLO
>
> Do you want to dance with me?

She smiles up at him, suddenly vulnerable.
He jumps down and spins her around. Then turns and starts to run up the wall. One, two, three steps – defying gravity. And then falls on his knees at her feet. She reaches out to him.

But the phone rings, piercingly, breaking the spell. Pablo turns away, his back to SP, murmuring into the phone.

> PABLO
> *(French and Spanish)*
>
> Hello? . . . Yes?
> I didn't know what time it was. Where are you? Okay.

OUTSIDE PABLO'S APARTMENT (PARIS) – NIGHT

Pablo and SP run down the staircase and out in the street outside his apartment building.

> SP
>
> Are you doing anything special for New Year's Eve?

> PABLO
>
> I don't know.

SP
(*hesitantly*)

Maybe we could go out dancing . . . or . . . if you want . . .

Pablo shrugs. He seems distracted.

PABLO

Yes . . . yes.

SP

Where shall we meet? At my hotel? Or . . . here, or . . .?

Pablo's mobile phone rings. He reaches into his pocket and switches it off.

PABLO
(*vaguely*)

Yes . . .

They move towards each other as if to kiss.
But then hold each other close, instead.
A little something has crept into the atmosphere.
Something wary.

HOTEL ROOM (PARIS) – NIGHT

INTERTITLE: THE SEVENTH LESSON

SP is preparing to go out.
Selecting an outfit.
Selecting earrings.
Looking at herself in the mirror, scrutinizing herself like a stranger.
And then humming happily.

OUTSIDE PABLO'S DOOR (PARIS) – NIGHT

SP rings Pablo's doorbell.
She looks fresh, eager and female, and dressed up for a night out.

No reply.

She practises a little tango step outside his door, as she waits.
And then, puzzled, she rings the bell again.

GAMES HALL (PARIS) – NIGHT

Pablo dives into an amusement arcade.
Blaring noise and flashing lights. Banks of screaming electronic screens.
Mechanical gunshots, firing over and over.

Pablo stands playing a solo game with a pinball machine in a kind of
hypnotic trance.
SCORE! SCORE! shouts the machine at him, neon winking. And
then: TILT!
Pablo throws a cigarette into his mouth, drags on it, and then, for a
moment, looks away from the flickering screen.

STREET OUTSIDE PABLO'S APARTMENT (PARIS) – NIGHT

SP walks slowly out of the shadows outside Pablo's building. A group of
New Year's Eve revellers run past, noisily, holding fireworks.

She turns and stares up at the dark windows. And then stands
immobile, in the road, for a brief eternity.

HOTEL ROOM (PARIS) – NIGHT

SP lies in bed in her hotel room staring into the darkness as car horns
blare and fire-crackers burst in the street outside.

And then the telephone rings.
She turns on the light and slowly picks up the phone.

> SP
> (*French*)
> (*quietly*)

Yes. I waited where we said. No, I'm *sure* we said . . . Okay,
okay. It doesn't matter. Goodnight.

She turns off the light briskly and lies on her back, staring again into the
darkness.
Silence.
And then there is a knock at the door.

> SP
> (*French*)

Who's there?

SP opens the door. There is Pablo, standing in the bare, dimly lit corridor, holding his mobile phone playfully in his hand.
He smiles, disingenuously.
SP crawls back between the sheets. Pablo closes the door and stands, leaning against the wall.

PABLO

You are angry?

SP

No, no. I'm sad.

PABLO

Why?

SP

Because . . .

She hesitates, scrutinizing his face for a moment. Then sighs.

In any case I was going to say . . .

PABLO

What?

SP
(French)
(gesturing deliberately)

That we should define our relationship more clearly. Set some limits.

PABLO
(French)

Okay. I agree . . .

SP

Oh.

Something has crept, unbidden, into SP's face. Disappointment.

INTERTITLE: THE EIGHTH LESSON

Pablo sits down in a chair.

                              PABLO
                            (*French*)
You know Sally, I wanted also to say something . . .

                               SP
                            (*quietly*)
Hmm?

                              PABLO
                            (*French*)
Yes. I've had a difficult experience before – when I mixed the
personal and the professional.

                               SP
                            (*French*)
                           (*casually*)
Oh yes?

                              PABLO
                            (*French*)
Yes. It's dangerous.

                               SP
                            (*French*)
                          (*dubiously*)
It can be.

                              PABLO
                            (*French*)
Everything can be destroyed.

They fall silent.
Pablo crosses the room and sits on the edge of the bed.

                              PABLO
                            (*French*)
You know, I think it's better to sublimate the attraction into
the work.

SP smiles.
Pablo looks at SP's face. Impenetrable. She's making it impenetrable.

You understand me?
To sublimate . . .

                               40

SP

Oh yes, yes, I understand.

PABLO

I think it's interesting to do that.

SP
(*dryly*)

Very interesting.

Silence, again.
And then Pablo falls onto the bed, stretching out beside SP, his back towards her.

PABLO

Sally, I really have to keep a distance.

He closes his eyes.

SP looks at his immobile form. His back gently rising and falling as he breathes in sleep.
Eventually she bends over him, reaches out and switches out the light.
Then lies down and looks at his body, sprawled unconscious beside her.
And then turns away, with a little sigh, eyes wide open in the darkness.

PABLO'S APARTMENT (PARIS) – DAY

INTERTITLE: THE NINTH LESSON

Pablo and SP are rehearsing.
Pablo is pushing SP. Really pushing her.
Criticizing. Finding fault.
The work has moved onto another level.
He's not treating her like a pupil any more, but like a partner. He's in pursuit of perfection, and so is she. But she is coming up against her limits and against her difficulties, physically and psychologically.

PABLO
(*French*)

More fluid. Let go! Less tension . . . just let go. Stop thinking. Don't *do* anything.

                    SP
                (*French*)
I'm *not* doing anything!

                  PABLO
                (*French*)
You are. You're blocking . . . you're leaning on me. You're
using too much force. Just centre yourself.

He leads her, repetitively, into a turn.

Why are you moving your head?
Follow me *here*. Stay *here*.

*He gestures in front of his body, and then turns away from her in disgust
as she stumbles.*

                    SP
                (*French*)
            (*groping angrily for words*)
Is it possible for you to encourage me more than . . . you
criticize me all the time. I'm *trying* . . . I'm really trying.

                  PABLO
                (*French*)
You could simply let go . . .

                    SP
              (*mimicking him*)
Let go, let go, let go! I'm trying to let go!

                  PABLO
                (*French*)
Yes, I know. I know.

They look at each other. Impasse. Then SP shrugs.

                    SP
                (*French*)
All right. I'll let go.

They both smile.
But he finds fault immediately.

                     42

                              PABLO
                            (*French*)
        You're doing it alone. You're doing it alone. Wait for me.

*SP puts her head in hands despairingly and starts crying. Pablo watches
her silently, and then takes the remote control device out of his pocket.*

Music.
A fast, driving joyful milonga (Milonga de Mis Amores).
Pablo invites SP into his arms in a conciliatory gesture.
They start to dance.

DANCE SALON (PARIS) – NIGHT

The same music continues.
*But now Pablo and SP are dressed up for a night out, still dancing the
milonga, weaving in and out of other couples in the crowded Parisian
dance salon where once they had danced alone.*

*When the music ends, they sit down at a table, occupied by a tall
English man, a tango aficionado.*
The English man turns to Pablo, ignoring SP.

                         ENGLISH MAN
                           (*Spanish*)
        Very good.

Pablo nods, politely.

                              PABLO
                           (*Spanish*)
        Thank you.

And then, there, at the other end of the hall, is Pablo's ex-partner.
A low murmur ripples through the salon.

*Pablo gets up, nonchalantly, without saying a word to SP, and crosses
the floor.*
*SP is left sitting at the table with the English man. He watches
attentively as Pablo holds his ex-partner tenderly and kisses her,
lingeringly, on the cheek.*

                         ENGLISH MAN
        You're English, aren't you?

                               43

SP

(slightly distracted)

Yes. Yes, I am.

A fast intense tango begins (Pensalo Bien).

ENGLISH MAN

Do you know this song? It's called *Pensalo Bien*. It's really rather interesting.

He starts translating the lyrics.

'Think hard before you take this step.
Because once you've taken it, there may be no turning back.
Think hard, because I've loved you so much,
And you've thrown it away,
Perhaps for another love.'

He smiles; an ironic, muscular smile which leaves his eyes fixed to SP's face, studying her reaction.
SP smiles politely, but her attention is elsewhere.
On the other side of the crowded salon Pablo and his partner are now dancing together, close, sensual, and fluid.

And then the English man invites SP onto the floor. He moves stiffly, crushing her hand in his as Pablo and his partner glide obliviously past them.

STREET (PARIS) – NIGHT

SP and Pablo are walking along a wide boulevard in the Pigalle district in the cold night air, as the neon lights of sex shops and strip shows flash behind them.

PABLO

You were jealous.

SP

No. No, I wasn't.

They walk on, in and out of the shadows, in and out of the pools of light falling from the street lamps.

Really not?

SP

No . . .

    All right, I was jealous. But not in the way you think. Really.

    I'm jealous of the contact we had before. I miss it.

She stops and pulls her coat tighter around her as she looks at him, quizzically.

    Anyway, aren't *you* ever jealous?

Pablo shakes his head.

PABLO

Never. I'm not a jealous person.

They walk on. SP watches him, smiling.
Eventually he catches her eye and stops.

PABLO

All right, all right. I can be jealous. *Very* jealous. But I choose not to be. I don't want all that again. I don't want violence. I don't want broken hearts. I don't want dramas.

They walk on.

PABLO'S APARTMENT (PARIS) – DAY

Pablo is leading SP into a jump.

PABLO
(*French*)

Straightaway! And *up!* More direct!

He lifts her into the same jump, over and over again.

    Be more prepared . . . More direct . . .

SP looks at him puzzled, as she tries again.

SP
(*French*)

No?

45

He adjusts her arm, infinitesimally.

>   PABLO
>   (*French*)
> No, don't move your arm . . . It's . . . it's . . . no, yes, there!

*SP jumps, again, but stumbles at the end. They move apart and look at
each other.*
Pablo gestures upwards.

> There's a moment, as if it stops . . . you should stay there.

He mimes a moment of suspended animation in the air above him.

> That's the idea.

SP points up into the air.

>   SP
>   (*French*)
> Stay there?

>   PABLO
>   (*French*)
> Yes.

SP shrugs.
And they continue.
Over and over again. But Pablo interrupts the jump repeatedly.

>   SP
>   (*French*)
> Why do you keep stopping?

>   PABLO
>   (*French*)
> Because *you* are stopping.

>   SP
>   (*French*)
> No, I'm not stopping! I'm ready!

>   PABLO
>   (*French*)
> No, you're stopping.

Let's go! There, that's it.

A good jump, finally.

                              SP
                          (French)
Was that better?

                            PABLO
                          (French)
A lot better.

They laugh.

BACKSTAGE AND ON STAGE (PARIS) – NIGHT

*Pablo and SP, dressed in stage clothes, are hurrying out of a dressing
room along a dark corridor, down some stairs, towards the sound – the
buzz – of an audience. The space closes and opens around their
backviews as they descend towards the noise, towards the light.*

*As they reach the wings Pablo takes SP's hand. They look at each
other.*
*And then burst, suddenly, out of the murky backstage darkness, onto the
enormity of the stage.*
Blinding, blinding footlights and the blaze of the follow spot.
*Applause from the dark cavernous space out there, somewhere beyond
the lights, somewhere beyond the spotlight – or searchlight, that bears
down on them. SP looks into Pablo's face. Eager. Afraid. Excited.*

*And then the music begins. A relentless, furiously rhythmic tango (La
Yumba).*
They start to dance.

All is glowing, phosphorescent, furious.
A blur of light and sound.
Pablo's eyes glowing like dark coals.

*The steps get more and more complicated. SP frowning with
concentration as she steps, kicks, swivels, jumps, turns.*
*Pablo at the centre of the vortex, SP running around him. She has
crossed over into his world. He leads, she follows.*

A final flurry of movement – a leap, suspended, somehow for a moment

47

in the air –
And then it is over.

They bow. SP turns towards Pablo breathlessly, expectantly, as the
applause washes over them. But he looks at her coldly. He gestures to
her to leave the stage. SP runs off as Pablo takes one last bow.

BACKSTAGE (PARIS) – NIGHT

SP and Pablo are hurrying back up the stairs and along the long dark
corridor towards the dressing rooms.

>   SP
>   (*breathless*)
>
> Well?
> What do you think?

Pablo quickens his pace.
SP runs to catch up.

>   SP
>
> Pablo? . . . Pablo? . . .

PABLO
(*quietly furious*)
You have to give up all the ideas you ever had about what it
means to be strong on stage.
You are confusing strength with tension.
You have to be calm to be strong.
You have to be slow to be quick. Everything else is from the
past, and you have to throw it *all* away.

*SP, flushed, breathless, wounded, as she hurries along the corridor
behind him.*

DRESSING ROOM (PARIS) – NIGHT

*Pablo crashes into the dressing room and sits down, angrily.
SP falls into her chair at the other end of the room.*

PABLO
Nothing!

SP
(*to herself*)
Oh God . . .

She is crying quietly, her head cradled in her arms.

PABLO
You should do *nothing* when you dance. Just *follow. Follow.*
Otherwise you block my freedom to move. You destroy my
liberty. And then I cannot dance. I *cannot* dance. I can do
nothing.

And then SP lifts her head and quietly starts to respond.

SP
And *you*, Pablo?
You danced as if I wasn't there. Like a soloist.

PABLO
No.

SP
Yes. It was like meeting a stranger on the stage. I couldn't
find you any more. You weren't with me.

49

You were out *there*, with *them*.

She gestures, indicating an imaginary public.
Pablo smiles to himself. Smiles in agreement.

I feel as if I've lost you.
Where are you?

Pablo is calmly looking at himself in the mirror.

PABLO

I am *here*.

SP gestures angrily, knocking a glass of water onto the floor.

And then the door opens.

A group of Pablo's friends, tango aficionados, crowds into the dressing room and clusters admiringly around Pablo, showering him with compliments.
SP turns her head away and dries her eyes.

A woman crosses the dressing-room towards SP, leans over her, and smiles an artificial smile.

> WOMAN
> (*French*)
> (*quietly*)

You were really very good . . .

A pregnant pause.

> . . . for the first time. Very good.

SP avoiding Pablo's eyes as she throws on a coat and leaves the room.

ON STAGE (PARIS) – NIGHT

SP walks slowly out from the wings onto the deserted stage and stares out into the silent, empty auditorium.

STREETS (PARIS) – NIGHT

SP walks angrily through the dark deserted streets. On and on.

She passes a phone box.
And then stops, suddenly.

BAR AND INT. PHONE BOX (PARIS) – NIGHT

Pablo is surrounded by partying friends; beautiful women and sycophantic men, laughing and drinking and making merry.

Pablo's mobile phone rings.
He reaches into his pocket, pulls it out, and turns away from his friends.

> PABLO
> (*French*)

Hello?

SP is crying into the phone in the phone box in the dark deserted street.

> SP
> (*French*)

Why are you afraid of me?

> PABLO
> (*French*)
> (*whispering*)

I am not afraid of you. I'm afraid of your weakness.

SP stops crying abruptly.

> SP
> (*French*)

What weakness?

> PABLO
> (*French*)

Your emotional weakness.

> SP
> (*French*)

I'm not weak. I'm *expressive.*
You think I could direct films and be *weak*?

Pablo is walking away from his friends, towards the corner of the bar.

> PABLO
> (*French*)

I haven't seen you direct.

> SP
> (*muttering angrily*)

That's because you wouldn't know it if you saw it.

                    PABLO
                    (*French*)
What?

                     SP
                   (*French*)
                  (*pointedly*)
I said, you don't know how to recognize what I do.

                    PABLO
                   (*French*)
                 (*sarcastically*)
I have eyes too. I haven't seen you do anything.

                     SP
                   (*French*)
               (*increasingly angry*)
You don't know how to use your eyes.
You're only interested in being looked *at*. Not at *looking*.
That's why you don't *see*. And that is why you know *nothing*
about *cinema*.

                    PABLO
                   (*French*)
               (*shouting viciously*)
And you know *nothing* about *tango*.

                     SP
                   (*French*)
                  (*shouting*)
And you know nothing about *me*.

                    PABLO
                   (*French*)
Maybe I don't *want* to know any more.

                     SP
                   (*French*)
Then I suppose it's over between us.

                    PABLO
                   (*French*)
What is?

                      53

SP
(*French*)

Exactly.

PABLO
(*French*)
(*bitterly*)

You have been using me to live out your little fantasy.

SP
(*emphatically*)

No. No. It's *you* who's been using me.
You never really wanted to dance with me. That's clear. You
have been humouring me, so that one day I might put you in
a film and make you into a *star*.

PABLO
(*French*)

Oh sure, sure.

SP

That's all you want, isn't it?

PABLO
(*French and Spanish*)
(*sarcastically*)

Yes, yes. Of course. And what else? What else?

SP
(*tearfully*)

There's only one thing left to say. Goodbye.

SP hangs up decisively.
Pablo switches off his mobile and hurls it to the ground.

*SP leaves the telephone box and walks slowly into the distance along the
dark empty street.*

CHURCH, ST SULPICE (PARIS) – NIGHT

INTERTITLE: THE TENTH LESSON

*SP is walking through the cool, shadowy church at St Sulpice; her face
ravaged, drained.*

She looks up. And then stands, immobile, in front of a huge painting by Delacroix of Jacob wrestling with the Angel.

She stands and she stares.
Jacob and the Angel – in a tango hold – wrestling in a dark valley through a long night.

> SP
> *(voice-over)*
> Pablo. Are you there?
> Perhaps not. Well, I want to tell you a story . . .

PABLO'S APARTMENT (PARIS) – DAWN

Pablo is sitting at the table, staring into space, listening to SP's voice on his answering machine.

> . . . It's a Jewish story. Jacob was alone in a valley, and there he met a stranger. They started to fight. They fought and wrestled through a long, long night. But as dawn broke Jacob realized that he could never defeat the stranger . . .

PHONE BOX OUTSIDE ST SULPICE (PARIS) – DAWN

SP is speaking softly into the telephone in a phone box by a fountain outside the church.

> . . . Because the stranger was an angel. Or God. Or perhaps, all along Pablo, Jacob had simply been wrestling with himself. It's dawn now . . .

A line of little girls dressed in white confirmation dresses is filing past the phone box, into the church. Little brides of Christ, their white veils covering their faces.

PABLO'S APARTMENT (PARIS) – DAWN

> . . . and I want to stop fighting. I want to begin again with you. I'm at St Sulpice. If you get this message, please come.

Pablo looks away and shakes his head.

CHURCH, ST SULPICE (PARIS) – DAY

SP is standing inside the church again under the painting in a dusty beam of morning sunlight.

Pablo appears beside her, quietly. They take each other's hands.
Then Pablo looks up at the painting. He pauses momentarily, and then instinctively takes up the position of the Angel.
SP smiles and then presses herself against him like Jacob, burying her face in his chest.

But then she slowly disentangles herself from the hold and looks up into his face.

> SP
> I've been following you in the tango, Pablo. But to make a film, you have to follow me. Are you ready?

FOUNTAIN OUTSIDE ST SULPICE (PARIS) – DAY

Outside the church, Pablo and SP walk slowly past the roar of the fountain.

SP trails her hands in the water.

And then lifts her hand and trickles water over Pablo's head.
A baptism.
Pablo looks at SP and then does the same to her.
It's a truce.

SP gazes tenderly at Pablo and then slowly bends down and buries her face in the water.

There, suddenly, in glowing colour, is a small floating figure, curled up underwater in a foetal position, and the pulsating sounds of the interior of a body.

And now the figure opens and floats up, up through the turquoise water towards a vast, spreading redness. It is Pablo, swimming in his stage costume, the tailcoat spreading out behind him like fins.
The sound of a heartbeat becomes the sound of . . .

TAXI (BUENOS AIRES) — DAY

. . . windscreen wipers pulsing across a rain-lashed windscreen.
SP and Pablo are sitting in a taxi in Buenos Aires driving through a tropical rain storm.
The taxi slowly comes to a halt. The noise of the rain on the car roof is deafening.

SP

Do you feel as if you're coming home?

PABLO

I don't know. Perhaps.

SP studies his profile and then turns away and looks out at the solid sheet of rain cascading down the windows of the car.

*And then comes the crackling sound of music on the car radio (*Milonga de mis Amores*).*
SP smiles at Pablo and opens the door of the taxi.

STREETS (BUENOS AIRES) — DAY

SP steps out of the taxi into the rain. She gestures invitingly to Pablo. He climbs out after her and they start to dance.

Drenched, saturated, splashing speedily through the gutters – skipping, twisting, spiralling.

The last of the tension between them finally washes away as they dance their milonga in the rain.

Soaked to the bone, they stop and throw their arms around each other.

SALON (BUENOS AIRES) – NIGHT

A dance salon, where the same music continues.
SP and Pablo enter the crowded, smoky dance hall side by side.
One by one the elderly couples come up to Pablo and greet him like the prodigal son. Hugging him, looking at him with pride, affection, respect, awe, tender ownership.

The master of ceremonies announces Pablo's presence over the booming sound system as people crowd around Pablo, edging SP aside.

> MASTER OF CEREMONIES
> (*Spanish*)
> Ladies and gentlemen, after seven years, our very own little Pablo Veron is back. A big round of applause for the great success of Pablito Veron!

A huge round of applause.
Pablo stands and raises his arms like a boxer acknowledging the crowd before a fight, and then is borne away by the crowd.
SP sits, alone at a table, looking about her as Pablo floats away on a wave of recognition and remembrance, swallowed up once more by his world.

And then Carlos appears.

He takes SP's hand and then they are on the dance floor together, finishing the same milonga that she had begun with Pablo in the rain.

Pablo's eyes flicker in their direction. For the first time, anxiety fleetingly passes across his face.

GUSTAVO'S STUDIO (BUENOS AIRES) – DAY

Gustavo and Fabian stand side by side in Gustavo's tiny studio. Pablo is sitting slumped in a chair.

GUSTAVO

What kind of film?

SP

I don't know yet. I'm in the middle of working it out.

Gustavo is smiling. Just a little warily.

FABIAN

With the three of us? Together?

Fabian looks from one to the other with an expression of studied innocence. SP turns to look at Pablo. He is already looking at her. He gets up and ambles over to the mirror and then swiftly executes a series of perfect pirouettes – ending by blowing himself a kiss.

FABIAN
(*grinning broadly*)

Is he a star, or what?

They slap hands, playfully; laughing.

The atmosphere has broken. The hierarchy has been established. And then the three men start playing together. Friends and rivals. Slapping, pushing, joking.
SP is handed from one to the other as they take it in turns to demonstrate steps, laughing and talking in Spanish.

And then they start showing steps directly to each other. They become lost in their rivalrous excitement. Men together. SP has become invisible, a presence. She walks slowly to the corner of the room and sits on the floor.

At first she watches them. But then her expression changes. She slowly turns and looks away from them. Looks into the space inside her head. But without her gaze something is missing. The men start to lose control without her appreciative attention. Pablo takes Fabian to show a particularly violent turn and he crashes into a mirror, waking SP from her reverie.

FABIAN

We're gonna have to find a bigger place if we are going to work with you, Sally.

61

The men laugh.
And SP laughs with them.

PARK (BUENOS AIRES) – DAY

Pablo and SP are walking in the sunshine through a small dusty park
by a lake.

> PABLO
> (*French*)
> You really don't know what kind of film it will be?

> SP
> (*French*)
> Not yet.

> PABLO
> (*French*)
> Then what did you tell the producers?

> SP
> (*French*)
> (*smiling*)
> Lies.

They laugh, together, conspiratorially.

INTERTITLE: THE ELEVENTH LESSON

A professional dog-walker is struggling along the path towards them
pulling a dozen dogs on leads.

> PABLO
> But tell me, Sally, how many numéros will I have in the film?

> SP
> Numéros?

> PABLO
> Yes, er, dance numbers.
> That's what I do. No?

> SP
> It's not really a question of *numbers*. There'll be a story.

PABLO

With *dialogue?*

Another dog-walker is coming in the opposite direction. Another dozen dogs. Barking.

SP

Yes. That's what I'm going to write.

PABLO

Then I must take acting lessons. For my voice, no?

He strokes his throat as the dogs pant their way past them, straining against their leashes.

SP
(*smiling*)

There's nothing wrong with your voice.
It's a very good voice.

PABLO
(*eagerly*)

Really?

SP laughs at his eagerness, at his unusual display of vulnerability. Pablo suddenly looks hurt.

> You are mocking me.
> I have been teaching you how to dance, and you have been teaching me *nothing*.

SP sighs. The atmosphere has turned again.

SP
(*French*)

Okay, okay, Pablo. Do you want me to teach you something?

PABLO
(*French*)

Yes, of course.

They continue walking. A Hasidic Jew passes them, briskly walking in the opposite direction.

SP
(*French*)

Say to me: 'I am a dancer'.

PABLO
(*French*)

'I am . . .' Why? You know that already.

SP
(*French*)
(*laughing*)

Okay. Suppose . . . I write a scene where I am telling you something important for me . . . that I feel like a Jew for example. And I say to you – And you, Pablo? and you reply – I am a dancer. And then you pause and add: *And* a Jew.

Pablo looks puzzled.

PABLO
(*French*)

Yes – it's possible. I might say that.

SP
(*French*)
(*warming to her idea*)
And then, maybe, a tear rolls down my cheek, and then a tear rolls down your cheek.

She reaches out and strokes his cheek.
Pablo stares at her. Silently.

PABLO
(*French*)
A tear?

SP
(*French*)
Yes.

PABLO
(*French*)
But maybe I don't want to do that. Maybe I don't want to cry.

SP stares at Pablo.

SP
(*French*)
(*quietly*)
Anything else you don't want to do? Please do tell me now, because maybe I don't want you in the film.

PABLO
(*French*)
(*sarcastically*)
And maybe I don't want to be in your *little* film.

SP
(*French*)
(*slowly*)
Fine. Then maybe I'll start looking for someone else . . .

And then she talks, fast and furious.

Because of course, I haven't been doing anything this last year, have I? I haven't been watching you, preparing you,

creating a role for you in my head. I haven't been loving you.
As a director *and* as a woman. No. I've done almost nothing.
Except follow. Badly. Because it doesn't suit me to follow,
you see. It suits me to lead. And you can't deal with that.

*She walks away, angrily, leaving Pablo standing alone, staring after
her.*

HOTEL ROOM (BUENOS AIRES) – NIGHT

*SP is sitting on her bed, papers and photographs strewn around her,
sobbing, as if her heart were breaking.*
Water running from her eyes and nose.
*Her hands drift over the papers, lightly touching the pages and images
as she weeps.*

And then the phone rings, piercingly.
SP blows her nose and slowly picks up the phone.

SP
(*softly*)

Hello.

MOVIE EXECUTIVE
Hi, is that Sally?

SP
Yes.

MOVIE EXECUTIVE
You're on a research trip, right? For the new project?

SP
Yes, I'm in the middle of preparing it now.

MOVIE EXECUTIVE
So, how's it going?

SP
(*deliberately*)
Oh, fine. *Very* well.

MOVIE EXECUTIVE
It sounds kind of intriguing. It's a sexy subject. You could attract some big names, right?

SP
(*quietly*)
No.

MOVIE EXECUTIVE
No?

SP
No stars.

MOVIE EXECUTIVE
But why not, Sally? This is an idea that could take off. So why limit yourself?

SP listens blankly to the voice at the other end.

SP
I thought after the last film you might trust my decisions.

And then SP is lying on her back on the bed, staring up at the ceiling as the light falls.

TAXI (BUENOS AIRES) – NIGHT

SP is sitting in the back of a taxi which is weaving about through the traffic in the darkness.
Streaks of light and rain on the windows.
Reflection upon reflection. Glittery and dark.

The taxi driver watches her in the rear-view mirror, as she looks out of the window, listening to the music (Gallo Ciego) playing on the car radio.
She glances into the mirror and catches his eye.

SP

Gallo Ciego. Pugliese.

The taxi driver swerves, pulls on the handbrake, stops the car and turns round with an expression of astonishment.

TAXI DRIVER
(Spanish)

Where are you from?

SP
(Spanish)

London.

TAXI DRIVER
(Spanish)

And you know the names of our *tangos*?

SP
(Spanish)
(smiling)

Why not?

The taxi driver studies her face for a moment, shrugs, and then turns back to the wheel and lurches out into the traffic once more.

TAXI DRIVER
(Spanish)

You have to have lived, to have suffered, to understand the tango. No? . . .

They drive on in silence.

He continues to study her in the rear-view mirror.

Tell me, Miss, are you alone in our city?

SP smiles ironically to herself and softly leans her head against the car window as they speed through the night and rain.

DANCE SALON (BUENOS AIRES) — NIGHT

The same music continues, but now the sound fills a crowded dance hall. SP arrives, sits down at a table and looks around her.

Carlos is dancing with his partner.
But when he sees SP sitting alone he immediately abandons her and crosses the room to SP's table.

> CARLOS
> (*Spanish*)

Hello!

> SP
> (*Spanish*)

Hello.

> CARLOS
> (*Spanish*)

Is it true, Sally, that you're going to make a film about the tango?

SP smiles up at him.

> SP
> (*Spanish*)

Yes.

> CARLOS
> (*Spanish*)

With *Pablo*?

He shakes his head, muttering under his breath.
Then takes SP's hand and leads her out onto the dance floor.
He holds her tight and they start to dance; close, sinuous, and sensuous.

Pablo appears in the entrance to the hall and stands in the shadows.
He looks around and then sees Carlos and SP dancing together.

And then he's walking – fast – out onto the dance floor.
He takes a running punch at Carlos. Carlos recoils, winded. And then,
in a split second, it turns into play.
They shadow box for a moment, smiling. Man to man.
Then Pablo softly pushes Carlos aside and takes SP into his arms
proprietorially. They start dancing together.

Carlos returns to his table.
His partner gestures at him angrily.

Pablo and SP continue dancing, absorbed only by the music and with
each other until the dance comes to an end.

STREETS AND COURTYARDS (BUENOS AIRES) – DAY

Gustavo, Fabian, Pablo and SP cross a busy, noisy Buenos Aires street
in bright sunshine. And then enter a courtyard.

Fabian checks the address on a piece of paper and then rings a doorbell.
A woman opens the door.

> FABIAN
> (*Spanish*)
> Hello. Dance studio?

The woman frowns up at him in disbelief.
The door slams in his face.

Back out into the street; another building; another door.
An elderly couple peer out into the hallway.

> GUSTAVO
> (*Spanish*)
> Dance studio?

The couple point across the hall.
Pablo rings the bell and a large man in a singlet answers the door.
Music (Soñar y Nada Mas) is playing on a radio inside.

> PABLO
> (*Spanish*)
> Dance studio?

RUSSIAN MAN
(*Spanish*)

Yes!

ROOM (BUENOS AIRES) – DAY

And then they are being ushered into what may have been a small dance studio at some point in its history: but now the room is full of furniture. The large Russian man gestures at an area the size of a double bed.

This is it. I can rent you this half. It's perfect, no?

He twirls toward them in a clumsy pirouette.
They stare at him in disbelief, avoiding each others' eyes.

STREET AND LIFT (BUENOS AIRES) – DAY

Into the street again.
Gustavo and Fabian lead the way into the building and up the stairs.
SP follows, but Pablo pulls her into the lift and shuts the wrought iron gates behind them.

PABLO
(*French*)

What's going on, Sally?

SP
(*French*)

Nothing.

PABLO
(*French*)

But you seem different.

SP
(*French*)

We're working. Remember?

PABLO
(*French*)

But you seem absent, somehow.
Didn't you enjoy dancing with me last night?

They smile at each other as the lift rises, shadows dancing across Pablo's face.

WAITING ROOM, ABANDONED DEPARTMENT STORE (BUENOS
AIRES) – DAY

*Pablo, Fabian, Gustavo and SP stand in a row opposite a middle-aged
janitor in a large, bare waiting room.*

                    JANITOR
                    (*Spanish*)
        I don't think it's possible.

                    FABIAN
                    (*Spanish*)
        Are you sure?

                    JANITOR
                    (*Spanish*)
        Everything is closed. There is nobody here.

                    GUSTAVO
                    (*Spanish*)
        And if we come back later?

                    JANITOR
                    (*Spanish*)
                    (*shaking his head*)
        I don't think so.

SP turns to Gustavo.

                    SP
        We'll wait.

                    GUSTAVO
                    (*Spanish*)
        She says we'll wait.

The janitor shrugs and disappears.
Gustavo and Fabian fall, exhausted, into two armchairs.
Pablo lies sprawled on a sofa between them.

Stasis.

SP looks at the three men, at their inert bodies.
Finally, Fabian stirs and yawns.

> FABIAN
>
> Well, Sally, I think I'm gonna go home now.

> GUSTAVO
>
> Me too.

Something changes in SP's face.

> SP
> (*suddenly and quietly decisive*)
>
> No.

The men look at her and at each other.

> SP
>
> Pablo, set up a rhythm, and teach it to the others.

> GUSTAVO
>
> Right now?

> FABIAN
>
> Here?

Pablo smiles at SP.
His face suddenly comes alive.

And then there he is tapping out a phrase.
Gustavo and Fabian follow, tentatively at first, and then more
confidently. The three of them pound rhythmically backwards and
forwards across the room.
SP watches, smiling.

> SP
>
> Now, Pablo. Solo.

Pablo catches her eye, and then he's off.
Fabian and Gustavo continue to pound away in unison as Pablo flies
across the floor, the cross-rhythms building in complexity and ferocity.

And then Pablo crashes through a door, which opens into an immense,
dusty, abandoned space. The space fills with light and the sound of fast,
driving music (Libertango).

73

ABANDONED DEPARTMENT STORE (BUENOS AIRES) — DAY

Gustavo takes SP and dances out into the space with her.
And then passes her to Fabian.
Fabian dances with her and then passes her to Pablo.
And then they dance all four together. Intimate, rapid moves. Feet
darting between legs; SP held between them as they dance as one.
SP moves fluidly from one to the other as they spur each other on to
larger and more dramatic moves, inspired and freed by the dimensions of
the space.
Turns and jumps and lifts. It becomes wild and anarchistic and athletic.
Their energy, frustration, competitiveness and exuberance finally finding
form.

After the dance is over, the group walk slowly down a cavernous
stairway.
SP is with Fabian and Gustavo. Pablo trails behind on his own. SP
glances back at him.

INTERTITLE: THE TWELFTH LESSON

Fabian, Gustavo, Pablo and SP meander slowly down some stairs into a huge abandoned barber's shop, lined with marble and mirrors. Gustavo turns on the lights and they look around them. Then Pablo pulls SP aside, out of earshot of the other two.

PABLO

Tell me, Sally.

SP

Yes?

PABLO

Will I do some tap dancing in the film?

SP

Perhaps. Yes.

PABLO

When will it be definite?

SP sighs.

SP

When someone believes in *me*, the way I believe in *you*.

Silence.

PABLO

That means there's no money to make the film?

SP

Not yet.

PABLO

Then what are we doing?

SP

Doing it anyway.

SP smiles and turns away from Pablo in to the main room of the barber's shop where Fabian and Gustavo are dancing together to the melancholic strains of a lyrical tango (Bahia Blanca).

75

Gustavo takes SP in his arms and they dance a few steps, but Fabian interrupts them.

FABIAN
Listen Sally, aren't you tired?

He picks her up and carries her to a barber's chair.
Gustavo exaggeratedly dusts down the seat of the chair.

FABIAN
We have to take care of our queen.

SP laughs.
Fabian and Gustavo continue dancing together.
Pablo crosses the room and heaves himself up onto a child's chair, his feet dangling.
He sits, immobile, staring at SP in the mirror as she watches Gustavo and Fabian dancing together, taking it in turns to lead and follow.

Then SP glances away and her expression shifts.
She looks at Pablo's backview. She looks at him looking at her looking at the other men.
Then she crosses the room and stands beside him and they look at each other in the mirror.

PABLO
Are you looking at me?

SP
Yes.

PABLO
What do you see, Sally?

SP
I see you on the screen.

PABLO
Then you are not here with me. You have become a camera.

SP
(*tenderly*)
But that's how I love you, Pablo. With my eyes. With my work.

PABLO

Work. Only work?

And then they turn, slowly, to face each other.

SP

What else do you want?

PABLO
(*slowly, deliberately*)
I want to know why we met.

SYNAGOGUE (BUENOS AIRES) – DAY

An old man is opening the doors into a synagogue.
He ushers SP and Pablo inside.
They walk in and sit at the back on separate sides of the centre aisle.

SP is the only woman present.
Apart from her the right side of the synagogue is empty.
On the left side, a small group of men is praying in the front rows.

A cantor is singing in his high, wailing, joyous voice.

Pablo's eyes fill with tears.

Pablo and SP turn and look at each other – an open, full glance; tender and accepting.

DOCKS (BUENOS AIRES) – NIGHT

SP and Pablo are walking through the abandoned, derelict docks at night, the lights of the city twinkling in the distance, reflected in the water.
A row of immense cranes towers above their tiny figures.

Pablo is speaking in a soft, halting voice.

PABLO

Tell me, Sally. What does it mean to feel like a Jew? Because, you know, I don't really feel at home in a synagogue. And, of course, even less in a church.
(French)
And Sally, I don't really belong in France, but I don't belong here any more either. I am afraid.

SP
(French)

Afraid of what?

PABLO
(French)

Of being someone without roots. I don't know where I've come from or where I'm going. I'm afraid I will disappear without leaving a trace.

SP
(French)

Perhaps *that's* why we met.

SP looks at Pablo tenderly. He falls into her arms. And then, softly, as they hold each other, she starts to sing to him.

SP
(sings)

Where did you come from?
Where, oh where?
From earth, from water
From fire, or air?

78

They start to dance as she continues to sing:

> When we're dancing
> Then I'm sure
> I know I know you
> From before.
>
> You are me
> And I am you
> One is one
> And one are two.

And then, finally, they kiss.

The END CREDITS *roll up over the scene as they dance away into the distance – two small figures, under the cranes in a huge, derelict, industrial landscape.*
SP's song continues:

> Travelling man,
> Man in my heart
> Man on stage,
> Man of his art.

Swiftly speaking,
With his feet
I see you, I hear you,
There we meet.

Where eyes and ears
Receive the word,
Where what is spoken
Can be heard.

You are me
And I am you
One is one
And one are two.

One is one
And one are two
You are me,
I am you.

POSTSCRIPTS FROM BEHIND THE SCENES

What follows are two pieces of writing generated at very different stages of the creation of the film. The first, titled 'Tango Lessons' I wrote immediately on my return from my first trip to Buenos Aires, *before* I had any conscious idea that this subject might become a film. The second 'The Archivist goes to Buenos Aires' was written during a pause in the shoot, after five weeks of filming in Paris, while I was in the throes of rewriting the sections of the film set in Buenos Aires. The nature of the story and the fact that the main parts were to be played by non-actors necessitated an openness to changes of direction as the shooting progressed. Tango is an improvised dance and this film had to be made in a way that echoed its mercurial spirit. But this was extremely demanding for everyone involved.

At such moments – alone in a hotel room at night in Buenos Aires, knowing that an entire production team and crew were waiting in a state of enforced paralysis for new script decisions – I would call on my old friend and adviser the archivist, a character who regularly appears during all my darkest writing hours to help clarify murky situations or states of mind. He helps me to ask the right questions and always puts me in my place if I am getting lost in generalizations, irrelevancies, hubris, or, more frequently, doubt.

First steps

After a few days and nights in Buenos Aires, I realize that as a city it reminds me of Paris mixed with New York, Moscow-style. It has some of the architectural beauty of Paris without any of its chic vanity. It has the cultural energy and long, straight, neon-lit avenues of New York without its egocentricity. It has the shabbiness of Moscow and the atmosphere of a city that has survived terrible political turmoil and repression. But this is not Eastern Europe – it is Latin America.

And bubbling away at the heart of the city is the beat of the tango. Every night of the week you can, if you wish to, dance until dawn. Entering into the world of the tango – as a visitor, an outsider, a gringo tango tourist – I am welcomed and taken to its bosom like a long-lost friend or even family. The music reaches into me – the lyrics express a kind of desperate extremity that has no voice in English culture – and the dancing lifts me to a state of rapturous joy.

Each day I take two or three lessons and each night go out to dance at two or three 'milongas' (dance halls). The lessons take in the full spectrum of the tango as it manifests now, from the original authentic 'milonguero' style – minimal, close-hold salon dancing where the couple focuses exclusively on each other and enters into an entirely private world governed by subtle signals – to the theatrical, sometimes extravagant style designed to be seen, to show off both partners to maximum effect and to take the moves to their own extremities of speed, virtuosity and grace. And somewhere in between lie the tango philosophers, epitomized by Gustavo Naveira, who understands both worlds, loves the history and feels the essence of the tango, and also shines brilliantly in the improvised vocabulary that at its most eloquent becomes astonishingly agile and continuously unexpected.

At night in the milongas, Jeff (my host and guide in Buenos Aires) and I watch riveted as couples in their fifties, sixties and seventies step onto the dance floor and start to move. A portly man in a grey suit with a grey bushy moustache and red swarthy

face, accompanied by his elderly plump wife, her swollen legs
packed into twinkly gold shoes, take the floor and astonish me
with their gazelle-like grace and lightness of touch. Turning,
gliding, pausing, kicking, swivelling, in perfect unison, with
perfect mutual understanding and a visible respect and
compassion for each other's qualities and frailties and strengths –
this is how to grow older.

For the tango is a dance that matures with age. It's no respecter
of youth and thinness – though those have their place too. The
young dancers, limber and athletic, also twizzle their own way to
heaven. But here in the milongas – which are large, usually shabby
dance halls, perhaps decorated with some balloons and tinsel, the
mournful, joyful strains of the tangos bursting out of the crackling
sound systems – this is where the working people – bent, fat,
balding, be-wigged, poured into Lycra mini-dresses, squeezed
magnificently into pointy shoes, bosoms thrusting, pot-bellies
grandly presiding – this is where the tango glows like a testament
to survival and graceful hope in the face of the ravages of ageing,
political repression and the apparent meaninglessness of daily life.

Here the ordinary becomes extraordinary, and the kitsch
becomes beautiful. Here the grotesque become adorable and the
misfits find a place; here the has-beens become somebodies; here
the humans become gods.

ON FOLLOWING

In the tango, as in most social dances for couples, one person
leads and the other follows. It is the norm for the man to lead and
for the woman to follow. In Europe and North America, where
nothing is taken for granted when it comes to gender definition,
this is seen either as problematic, or, usefully, as an opportunity
for women to learn and experience both roles. In Argentina, it is
an accepted division of labour and implies nothing derogatory for
either sex.

As someone who leads for much of her working life (as a
director), the opportunity to learn what it means to follow was a
blessing.

Someone once said that Ginger Rogers did everything that Fred
Astaire did, only backwards and wearing high heels. That is

certainly true of following in the tango. Far from being an expression of passivity it is one of acutely skillful manoeuvering, at high speed, often backwards. But this is just the obvious part of the form. And the form is based on a contract. One person (the leader, whether male or female) chooses and shapes the steps of the dance, the other (the follower) responds so instantaneously that it is as if the two dancers move as one in an extraordinarily elaborate choreography. The best leaders make their partners look and feel like creatures of consummate grace, beauty, strength and skill. The best followers make their partners look and feel the same. Each enhances the other's sense of self and feeling of freedom.

The joy of being a follower is that it demands a complex and sometimes paradoxical series of qualities. You must be both completely centred and balanced, yet able to move at a moment's notice in any direction. You must be completely in control of your body, yet surrender control of where you are going. You must be completely grounded yet free enough to feel that you are flying. You must be toned enough to provide enough resistance to the leader so that he (or she) can direct you, yet be completely relaxed so that there is no obstruction. You must be completely mentally alert, yet your mind must be 'empty'. Above all, you must be completely in the present. Without the sheer now-ness you cannot follow at the speed and with the precision that is required.

Entering into this state of alert receptivity, I find the energy coiling in my abdomen like a spring, every anxiety banished from my mind, my ears open to every nuance of the music, my body responsive to every tiny pressure and touch of my partner until I feel that I *am* his body and he is mine. In other words, I enter a state of pure libidinous energy which I have only ever experienced either in love-making, in meditation, or in the rapturous moments when, either writing or singing or directing, all seems to unify and become itself at once, effortlessly.

The tango is often caricatured as kitsch eroticism – a couple clasping each other in a parody of twenties togetherness. That's the Europeanized public image of the tango. On home ground the sexuality is there, but it is sublimated. The moves do not imitate the sexual act. But they are sometimes violently quick or agile – wordless expressions of a life force when it connects two individuals. For above all, the tango is an expression of connectedness. You cannot dance tango alone.

Every time you take the dance floor with a stranger, you are entering an agreement to step over the precipice into the chasm between you. You negotiate the unsayable, you try to express the inexpressible. You give voice to the 'I and thou' that Buber wrote of. You use each opportunity, within the discipline and codes of the dance, to say 'I hear you'.

So, pretence is out of the question. You feel immediately if the partner is sensing you or is oblivious to your rhythm, your body. You sense immediately when your partner opens himself to you or closes against you. You communicate wordlessly – how far can I go with you? How deep can we reach into each other? Who are you? Can you feel who I am? And together you can, in some glorious moments, soar away to heaven. Then you go back to your seats, your hearts pounding. A little bow, perhaps; a nod, a thank you. The social codes safely contain the adventure that is at once sensual, athletic, musical and spiritual.

GUSTAVO

Almost every day I cross Buenos Aires to Gustavo's small mirrored first floor studio in the fabric district. He's sometimes late – still asleep at five in the afternoon after a very late night – and must be woken by a phone call. Then he arrives, a little shamefaced, at the local café bar where I am waiting. But a few moments later in the studio, once the music is playing, he enters into his unique form of concentrated teaching.

In my case, he senses intuitively that I will learn best kinetically. We hardly talk at all. We just dance, and dance, and dance. He glides and turns, this way and that, gently removing my arms if I press too much on his shoulder, very occasionally stopping to explain a move, but mostly teaching wordlessly through doing, through repetition. If I miss a step the first time, he will present another opportunity to catch it soon after. Heavy-lidded with concentration, his moustached face becomes Buddha-like. And like a good-natured monk, he laughs easily.

Some days into the week I arrive and say I need to talk. He nods graciously as I pour out my impressions – of different ways of dancing, of the roots of the tango, of the social and political meanings as they appear to me. He reaches for a pen and paper and starts to draw. Here is the twenties, and here the thirties. Here is the forties – the golden age of the tango – dominated by Petrolio. Here is the fifties – and now in the sixties the tango is dead. Only the Beatles exist. And in the seventies it is still dead – but now in the eighties it starts to come alive again. Copez becomes the king of tango. The tango spreads through the rest of world and is exposed to other influences. And now it is in a state of transition once more.

I ask him: where does the tango really manifest – on the dance floor, in the process of learning, or on the stage in a theatre? He replies: it was originally in the salon, it came alive in the eighties again on the stage, and now in the transition we are moving into something else. We are moving towards an unknown.

His own place in the picture is as a pedagogue, but also as an improviser, probably the best. He has a grasp of a seemingly endless vocabulary of possible moves and variations which make his dancing akin to the most inventively esoteric new music improvisers, but with the visual accessibility of a great variety performer. His conceptual hunger to examine the tango philosophically makes him a tango intellectual, but he is no dry academic – his joy when dancing is infectious, his appetite for dancing seems undimmed; and as a dance partner or teacher he is able to communicate accurately and without words in such a way that one feels seen and appreciated on a primal level.

'You must let yourself go,' he says to me, quietly, as we dance. 'Let your body go where it wants to.' 'Don't think about it too much. Just learn to relax.' As the lessons sink in, I find that if I relax, I have to stop criticizing myself. I start to feel good – fluid and graceful, on top of things without having to control them. Gustavo's work with me becomes the spine of the experience of Buenos Aires – a place to return to, the essential level of the tango, the place of revelation and transformation.

GRAZIELLA

We arrive at Graziella's apartment building in beautiful sunshine and ring the polished brass doorbell. A few minutes later she

87

appears, unlocks the door and ushers us towards the tiny lift. She is diminutive, unsmiling, with long dark hair and ample proportions. In her small, tiled room she gets Jeff and me to dance for a while, while she prowls about watching, smoking a cigarette, staring at my feet. Okay, okay. She leads me to a wall and the work begins. Slow motion, painful precision. The footwork starts again from scratch. Don't turn out. The knees always touch. She demonstrates, her legs and feet gliding like butter across the floor. And now! – she pulls my hips around – here! – every move of the feet is generated by activity in the pelvis. We graduate to boleos (where the hips rotate and one leg swiftly kicks behind, then returns like a yoyo to its original position – sometimes so fast it's like a blur) and ganchos (where you hook your leg around your partner's in a sudden swift embrace. Strong, yet relaxed).

After an hour and a half I am drenched in sweat and my legs are trembling. I stagger out into the light, my body flooded with memories of what it means to *train*. Not since my early twenties have I done this kind of precise, arduous physical work. And it brings with it a flood of painful memories: of broken dreams and unfulfilled promise as a dancer; of being hopelessly up against my own physical limitations (I did not start dancing until I was twenty-one). But she has also imbued me with hope. She seems completely undeterred by my relatively advanced years (attitude and musicality being much more important than age in the tango), and obviously glories in the attention to detail and pursuit of excellence for its own sake.

I remember suddenly what I always loved about dancing – the combination of vigorous endeavour, present timedness, and dedication to process – the sure knowledge that you never 'arrive', you are instead in a constant process of arrival. It is itself, and it is a metaphor: for learning, for living, for being.

JUAN CARLOS COPEZ

Jeff and I have been out dancing, as usual, until 4 a.m. At 5 a.m. after reading a couple more pages of *Heartbreak Tango* by Manuel Puig, I fall into a deep sleep, but wake, ragged and alert before 9.00. I get up and pad about in my socks in the grey morning light, warming up.

At 10.00 sharp the doorbell rings. The caretaker has recognized Copez. This gives Jeff some pleasure and reinforces his identity as a serious tango-ist, for he has arrived from New York some months earlier to dedicate all his energies to the tango. We get to work in the tiny empty room with its shiny dark wooden parquet floor.

'You're leaning on me! Stop leaning!' Copez falls backwards exaggeratedly as though I were a ten-ton truck mowing him down. I stumble and stiffen when he leads me into an unfamiliar step. 'No, no, no.' He shakes me like a sack of potatoes. 'Why? Why you're not following me?' I can choose to crumble and cry under the barrage of criticism, or rise to the master's instructions. I choose the latter. After half an hour I am apparently more on my own axis, though I *feel* as if I am leaning backwards. He is gliding around me like a panther – sleek, shiny with sweat. I am close to his dyed brown hair with its famous centre parting. I can see every line in his face. I can feel his worked body.

He demands that I both occupy my own space and take total responsibility for my own balance during all the moves, and yet simultaneously be completely relaxed and responsive to his every move and lead. 'Fifty, fifty – that's how we must be. The man, the woman, fifty, fifty. It's dialogue.' I realize that in order for him to glide, to glisten, to shine like the star he is, I must surrender my will and give him space. And yet he says, over and over, 'Be yourself!' And so it is. I surrender false controls and find another more flexible self.

He is a theatrical performer, even in this little room with only Jeff for an audience. He works full out, his expression as concentrated as it ever is on stage. An hour later he wipes himself down with a towel and packs his shoes away, then turns to me. Suddenly his face shows some vulnerability. 'Did you enjoy it? Did you?' I reassure him with praise and thanks.

Afterwards, though I am pale and tired, drunk with lack of sleep and steeped in a curious ambitious yearning, I feel suddenly, like a girl in early teenagehood, full of the memory of a vital childhood, bursting with fresh female hormones, open and receptive to an exciting world, on my own feet, but longing to be held. As the week progresses, this feeling grows and grows. I remember that I have a female body, and I love it. I start to glow and feel both

89

rounded and athletic. Muscles reappear in my legs that had
vanished years ago; my shoulders fall back into a long forgotten
alignment; my pelvis hangs free and strong from my spine. And
the learning curve is virtually vertical.

Ah, I think to myself. If only I could learn to live the way I
dance. If only I could learn to work (to write, to direct) without
pretension and self-consciousness, strong and sure and vulnerable
and open, all at once – sweating, working, at my own limits and
yet easy, flooded with pleasure. Ah, tango, be my teacher, be my
guide, and perhaps I will remember who I really am.

POST-SCRIPT

Towards the end of my stay, I agree to do a couple of newspaper
interviews. I had not managed to come over for the opening of
Orlando in Argentina, and it had been very well received. In the
first interview with *Clarín*, the biggest daily newspaper, after some
discussion about the nature of the tango and why I am here, the
interviewer asks me, 'But what has this to do with cinema?'

'Someone said the essence of cinema is movement,' I reply,
trying to remember who that person was. 'All directorial decisions
are also choreographic ones. Where the camera should be, and
should it be moving or still; where the bodies are, and what and
how they are communicating. Even the flicker of an eyelash in a
strictly realist piece of cinema is also a piece of choreography. And
film exists only in time – like dance. To understand movement, I
must move. And to make a musical – which I want to do
sometime – I must immerse myself in a culture which is itself
immersed in the language of dance and music. So I am here both
for my own pleasure and as a form of research for a film I want to
make one day.'

The relative clarity I am able to muster in an interview disguises
the deep crisis of identity I am in reality wrestling with. If I love to
dance *this much*, does this mean I should be a dancer? Can I be a
serious film-maker *and* whizz off to Buenos Aires to dance the
nights away? Just exactly what kind of being am I, that I can be so
relentlessly, monkishly dedicated to script-writing and cinema on
the one hand, then so hedonistically, libidinously immersed in the
tango a day later? And how is it that I can be so allergic to forced

sentiment and sloppiness on film, but then weep copiously and shamelessly at the tango lyrics which are a sheer over-the-top melodramatic expression of raw pain and longing? And how can I fight tooth and nail and with every brain cell at my disposal against female (and all other forms of) oppression – and then delight in wearing the slinkiest, most figure-hugging clothes and highest stiletto dance shoes I can find? I guess, like every other individual on earth, I am a complex bundle of contradictory identities and am simply fortunate enough to have the means to express some of them.

On my return to London, hallucinating with lack of sleep and the sheer intensity of the experience, I immediately go out dancing – and do so, compulsively, every night for the next few nights in an attempt to come down. It may not be quite the same in the Welsh Centre in the Grays Inn Road or in the back room of a pub in Brixton, but the aficionados dance and sweat together just the same.

I discover that my focus has shifted whilst I am away. With each new partner I aim to enable him or her to feel more free, daring and able than they have ever felt before. As I do this, and feel the difference it makes to them, I realize this is the gift I was given in Buenos Aires. They allowed me to feel more free, daring and able than I had allowed myself to experience for a long time. It's an infectious process.

First published by Faber and Faber in *Projections 4* in 1995.
© Sally Potter, 1995

The archivist goes to Buenos Aires

The archivist had been waiting, apparently for some considerable time, at the airport. Sitting on his small, somewhat shabby, but perfectly adequate suitcase in a cool marble hall.

Eventually SP turned up. Only two hours late. Is this one of the skills you have learned here? asked the archivist, not without irony. How very useful to have such a casual disregard for the clock. How very useful to be liberated from such tiresome constraints as punctuality and consideration for others. You must feel very – *free* – is that the word? SP apologized. It was the traffic, you see, on a Sunday, and it's raining, and there was a demonstration. Ah – not just one reason, but three, said the archivist. The gift of elaboration – is that a new skill also?

And then they were weaving in and out of the traffic along the long dusty roads into the city. The archivist coughed. Mmm – real city air. Not too fresh – that's good, he said. A real metropolis at last. His eyes were drooping. There's something soothing about such excessive noise and haste, he said. It induces a hypnotic sense of the arbitrariness of chaos. There is no disguising the primal disorder and so one is once more alone on a trajectory of chance and random happenings, in the face of which one can only enter into a state of acute passivity. Yes, indeed, most soothing.

He closed his eyes.

SP watched his face. Studied the familiar contours. Watched the gentle rise and fall of his chest under his uncomfortable-looking jacket. And then, for a moment, her face twitched with fear. The archivist seemed to have stopped breathing. It can't be. It can't be. A rush of love and appreciation and regret flooded through SP. How little I valued him, she thought, how I have abused his loyalty. How can I ever forgive myself – and then he breathed again. The breath of a child in sleep.

Later, in the hotel, they ate a meal of chips together in the wood-panelled dining room; an elderly waiter in smiling attendance.

Delicious, said the archivist. Exactly what I had in mind. Now tell me, my dear, why you have called me across the water. Not that I mind spending thirteen hours in an aeroplane, not at all. It is always interesting to experience *distance*. Especially when it is distilled through *time*. And especially when the time and space are mediated through both *air* and *night*. Do tell me. I am all ears.

And the archivist, blushing slightly, wiggled his ears. This made SP laugh, although it made her want to cry. It was so English, somehow, that this middle-aged man was prepared to pull out a little party trick, a joke against any possible remnants of dignity, in order to relax her. Once more she was struck by his generosity.

In all honesty, she began –

Oh don't bother with honesty, interrupted the archivist, that takes far too long. Besides which, lies are *far* more interesting. I was going to say, SP continued – But my dear, don't bother with what you *were* going to say. Just concentrate on what it surprises you to say. Just tell me some truly astonishing lies, at high speed.

SP sat in silence, for a moment, pondering on how to proceed. An alert silence which took in the dull roar of traffic in the streets outside, the soft tick of the watch clamped to the waiter's hairy wrist, the creaking of floor boards in the long shiny corridors of the hotel upstairs.

Finally she began to speak. And notice, immediately, that her voice had dropped a tone or two. It was a deeper, throatier voice. A softer, huskier, and yet more authoritative voice. The voice she had had when she was a little girl – rosy-cheeked, hard at play, shouting, laughing – telling the others what to do. Some had called it being a born leader. Others had called it bossy. Only gradually had she become aware of her qualities as they were given names by others. Precocious. Talented. And a liar. You can't possibly have written that by yourself, they had said of her poems and essays. Tell us the truth now – your father wrote it for you, didn't he? Tears in the toilets. Loneliness. Learning how to pretend not to know things. Learning how to act being a child. With the eyes and inner life of a grown soul, and the passions of an artist.

Well, said the archivist. I'm waiting.

You see, said SP, my character in this story is labouring under a curse.

Interesting, said the archivist. What curse?

The curse of talent, which dooms her to a life of solitude in which she is also the object of envy and rage.

Are you sure? asked the archivist gently. I don't wish to accuse you of hubris but is that really the nature of the curse?

How about the curse of loneliness? asked SP. How about the curse of longing? How about the curse of dissatisfaction? Or of doubt?

Ah. Doubt. Now here we are getting somewhere, said the archivist. Doubt is an interesting case. Less glamorous as a concept than – say – solitude. But more complex. It implies both engagement and conflict. Might I suggest you examine also the idea of courage?

Silence again.

Courage? SP seemed bewildered.

Courage, said the archivist softly.

The next day SP visited the archivist in his room. He had unpacked the boxes from his suitcase and was already wearing white gloves. It was noticeable, however, that he had dark rings under his eyes.

Did you stay up late last night? asked SP. Couldn't you sleep?

I couldn't resist stepping out, he replied. Well, to be frank, I went out dancing.

Dancing? You? SP couldn't hide her astonishment.

You seem surprised, said the archivist, obviously a little hurt. But those of us who spend a lifetime in the vaults inevitably develop a very strong sense of movement.

I don't follow, said SP.

Oh but you do, replied the archivist, tartly. Rather too well, I fear. And that is misleading for the men here. And confusing for them also. But as I was saying, there is no contradiction between my line of work and fancy footwork. On the contrary, they are merely two faces of the same research.

Research into what? asked SP.

The ephemeral, the archivist promptly replied. And then he started to open the boxes.

This is what you have been sending me, he said. I have received the same material several times, with only minor variations. He held the images up to the light – the white sunlight – of the window. It was an image of a woman crying. *Really* crying. As if her heart was going to break. River of water cascading from eyes and nose, pouring down her cheeks, dripping from her chin.

Why? asked the archivist. And by that I don't mean why is it here, but why are you resisting putting it into your story?

Doesn't it make her look too weak, too weedy, too feminine? asked SP.

On the contrary, said the archivist. It shows the extent of her passion, her longing, and her disappointment. And all without words.

Your character is dealing with loss. She is having a crisis. A profound crisis. Don't be tempted to gloss over that or trivialize it. Remember that in everyone's secret world, the desires and disappointments are far greater than they will ever admit, even to themselves. It is not a sign of weakness to have desires. It is not a sign of weakness to have doubts.

He opened another box.

This one too, is full of snippets which you keep generating and rejecting.

It's a kiss. A box of kisses. I would just like to say one thing to you about that. Screen kisses have a history which you ignore at your peril. On screen, unlike in life, they are a moment of closure. An aspect of the story is finished with a kiss. Because once the characters join mouths they no longer have anything to tell us.

I don't agree, said SP.

Ah. Interesting, said the archivist.

If she yields to his kiss, then the story *is* over, said SP. Because screen history tells us, in effect, that they get married and live happily ever after. If *he* yields to *her* kiss, then, on the contrary we know we're in trouble. Interesting trouble.

You have a point, said the archivist. But, if you want my advice, you shouldn't think too much about it. Just take yourself – and us – by surprise. Don't be too careful.

Okay – forgive my colloquialism but I also watched an American film on television rather late last night when I returned from the dance salon, and I always absorb these little expressions – okay – dancing can tell us a lot, but a kiss is just a kiss.

Let's move on, shall we?

The third box. Walking. Broken pavements. Dust. Dogs. Twenty dogs on leads all being walked by one young man. A professional dog-walker. In a dusty park. Another professional dog-walker coming in the opposite direction. Pablo and SP in the middle of it all, arguing. Again.

My goodness, these two do like to share conflict, don't they. It must be because they haven't got to the bottom of it. What is it they are really trying to say to each other? asked the archivist, apparently casual.

That they met a long, long time ago, said SP. Somewhere, once, before they were born. When they lived in other bodies in another country. And they made an agreement. An agreement which was broken, and for which they can never forgive each other.

What kind of agreement, asked the archivist?

They were betrothed, said SP.

Oh yes? asked the archivist. Are you sure?

They were entertainers. Child entertainers, said SP.

Are you sure?

They were lovers, said SP.

Oh yes?

Rivals, said SP.

Yes?

Silence. And then SP put her head in her hands. I don't know, she admitted finally. I just don't know.

Maybe you're looking too far back, suggested the archivist. How about last week? Last year? What agreement? What was broken?

The agreement, SP reluctantly spelt out, was very simple. And it was proposed by me. I proposed to Pablo that he could have anything he wanted. Anything. All he had to do was have the courage to dream. I spoke the unspeakable to him. A limitless horizon. I said to him – I recognize your ambition and I love your talent. To me it is a gift and a blessing. And I said, softly to him, like a lullaby; And I am the angel who has arrived in your life to help you realize your ambition, to make manifest your dream, to render visible your magic. All that I said to him. Perhaps not in those words. But I held out my hand to him and said – come.

And he said to me: You can come into the sanctuary of the dance and find yourself again. You can rest your feverish brain in the absorption of the physical. You can, for a moment, step out of your tiresome responsibilities and afterwards you will be refreshed. I can give you the secret of eternal youth and I can give you love.

And I said to him – I will make you into a movie star. And he said to me – I will make you into a great dancer. In my arms you cannot fail. And I said to him – And in my hands you can only succeed.

And for those moments each offered the other unconditional love, unconditional acceptance, and unconditional appreciation. It was bound to lead to trouble.

Not bad, said the archivist. A bit too long-winded. But not bad. Let's come at it from another angle. Why do you want to kill him, at this point? And he you?

SP laughed. It comes down to that, does it? Murder?

Not necessarily acted out, said the archivist. But the passion is surely there. We are dealing with the force of 'crimes de passion'. That which we love most, we end up hating. You can never possess him as a dancer. He is quicksilver. Mercury. He slips out of your fingers. And he can never hold you for it is you who is containing him – in a film – making his image, *creating* him, if you like. He is resisting you with all the force of a wild horse that is being broken. All the force of a painting that refuses to be painted, a book that refuses to be written, a film that refuses to be made. But which *will* be made. And it is in the face of that inevitability that he crumbles, finally. Because, in the act of being *written*, he has forgotten who he really is.

And in the act of writing him, and writing yourself, you have once more taken on the mantle of responsibility from which you initially took refuge in his arms. A place of refuge which he now denies you.

Admit it – you feel alone and tired. And without hope. Doomed to accept your own power. Doomed to feel an outsider of your life, of your sex, and even of your art. But never mind, dear. As my mother used to say, it's better than a life spent working the conveyor belt in a canned pea factory.

CREDITS

ADVENTURE PICTURES
presents
a co-production with
OKCK FILMS (Argentina)
PIE (France)
NDF/IMAGICA (Japan)
PANDORA FILM AND CINEMA PROJECT (Germany)
SIGMA PICTURES (Holland)
with the participation of
THE ARTS COUNCIL OF ENGLAND
THE EUROPEAN CO-PRODUCTION FUND (UK)
THE SALES COMPANY
and
EURIMAGES
MEDIEN-UND-FILMGESELLSCHAFT BADEN-WURTTEMBERG
NPS TV COBO FUND (Holland)

THE TANGO LESSON

Editor
HERVE SCHNEID
Costume Design
PAUL MINTER
Production Design
CARLOS CONTI
Choreography
PABLO VERON
Sound
JEAN-PAUL MUGEL
GERARD HARDY
Director of Photography
ROBBY MULLER
Co-producer (France)
SIMONA BENZAKEIN
Co-producers (Argentina)
OSCAR KRAMER
CHRISTIAN KELLER SARMIENTO

Produced by
CHRISTOPHER SHEPPARD
Written and directed by
SALLY POTTER

CAST

(*in order of appearance*)

SP	SALLY POTTER
Red Model	MORGANE MAUGRAN
Yellow Model	GERALDINE MAILLET
Blue Model	KATERINA MECHERA
Fashion Designer	DAVID TOOLE
Photographer	GEORGE YIASOUMI
Seamstresses	MICHELE PARENT
	CLAUDINE MAVROS
	MONIQUE COUTURIER
Bodyguards	MATTHEW HAWKINS
	SIMON WORGAN
Pablo	PABLO VERON
Pablo's Partner	CAROLINA IOTTI
Pablo's Friends	ZOBEIDA
	ORAZIO MASSARO
	ANNE FASSIO
	GUILLAUME GALLIENNE
	MICHEL ANDRE
	FLAMINIO CORCOS
Man at Tea Dance	HOWARD LEE
Builder	HEATHCOTE WILLIAMS
Waiter	JUAN JOSE CZALKIN
Gustavo	GUSTAVO NAVEIRA
Fabian	FABIAN SALAS
Shoe Man	HORACIO MARASSI
Salon Dancers	DAVID DERMAN
	OSCAR DANTE LORENZO
	OMAR VEGA
Carlos	CARLOS COPELLO
Olga	OLGA BESIO
Hotel Porter	CANTILO PEÑA
Movie Executive	MARIA NOEL
	FABIAN STRATAS
	GREGORY DAYTON

99

English Tango Fan	PETER EYRE
Woman in Dressing Room	EMMANUELLE TERTIPIS
Master of Ceremonies	RUBEN ORLANDO DI NAPOLI
Taxi Driver	TITO HAAS
Carlos' Partner	ALICIA MONTI
Woman Opening Door	MARIA FERNANDA LORENCES
Couple Opening Door	LUIS STURLA
	AMANDA BEITIA
Man Opening Door	MARCOS WOINSKI
Janitor	EDUARDO ROJO
Man at Synagogue	OSCAR ARRIBAS

CREW

First Assistant Director	WALDO ROEG
Casting Director	IRENE LAMB
Story Editor	WALTER DONOHUE
Script Supervisor	PENNY EYLES
Associate Producers	DIANE GELON
	CAT VILLIERS
Production Co-ordinator	ROANNE MOORE
Director's Assistant	AMOS FIELD REID
Production Assistant	MICHAEL MANZI
Production Secretary	ANGELA NEILLIS
Script Translation	ELIE ROBERT-NICOUD
Focus Puller	PIM TJUJERMAN
Clapper/Loader	OONA MENGES
Key Grip	RICHARD BROOME
Gaffer	CHRISTOPHER PORTER
Boom Operator	SOPHIE CHIABAUT
Wardrobe Supervisor	MICHAEL WELDON
Costume Makers	DOREEN BROWN
	JACKIE HALLATT
	GLEN HILLS
	PETER LEWIS
	JOHN KRAUSA
Men's costumes from	CARLO MANZI RENTALS
Costumiers	CHRISTOPHER WITT
	JOANNA RODERICK
Shoes made by	JAMES TAYLOR & SON
	MASSARO
Make-up Artists	THI-LOAN NGUYEN
	CHANTAL LEOTHIER

Wigs by	PETER KING
Stills Photographers	MOUNE JAMET, SYGMA
	GEORGUI PINKHASSOV, MAGNUM
	RICHARD KALVAR, MAGNUM
Production Lawyer	LAW OFFICE DIANE GELON
Entertainment Lawyer	MARIA VAZQUEZ KELLER
	SARMIENTO
	MARVAL, O'FARRELL & MAIRAL
Production Accountant	RICHARD HYLAND

PARIS CREW

Production Manager	PHILIPPE BESNIER
Location Managers	ERIC VIDART-LOEB
	DENISE CASSOTTI
Assistant Location Manager	MARIE-EVE DURAL
First Assistant Director	JEROME BORENSTEIN
Third Assistant Director	OONA SEILER
Production Coordinators	MARIE-LAURE COMPAIN
	FLORENCE FORNEY
Production Accountant	MARIE-NOELLE HAUVILLE
Assistant Accountant	SARAH PORTAL
Casting Director	FREDERIQUE MOIDON
Models Casting Director	PRUDENCE HARINGTON
Extras Casting Director	ALBERTE GARO
Co-Producer's Assistant	ALEXIS DELAGE-TORIEL
Production Assistants	OLIVIER MARTIN
	GUILLAUME DUNAND
	HELEN CHALANT
Assistant Art Directors	STEPHANE CRESSEND
	MARIANNA ZENTCHENKO
	FERNANDO CARDOSO
Prop Master	RENAUD COLAS
Construction Manager	GILLES LABOULANDINE
Head Carpenter	PATRICK WIDDRINGTON
Head Painter	DANIEL MAUVIGNIER
Painter	BERTRAND GUINNEBAULT
Swing Gang	MARC LE HINGRAT
	LUDOVIC DUCHATEAU
Wardrobe Assistant	IVONE TELES
Hairdresser	CHRISTIAN GRUAU
Grip	MICHEL STRASSER

Electricians	PATRICK GASCHE
	GILBERT SEYBALD
Steadicam Operator	JORG WIDMER
Camera Trainee	HOYTE VAN HOYTEMA
Stunt Supervisor	PATRICK CAUDERLIER
Stunt Woman	PASCALINE GIRARDOT
Special Effects Supervisor	CHRISTIAN TALENTON
Unit Driver	MIKAEL RICHARD
Catering	TRAITEURS DU VERN

BUENOS AIRES CREW

Line Producer	OSCAR KRAMER
Production Manager	DIANA FREY
First Assistant Director	CARLOS GIL
Second Assistant Director	RODRIGO CARVAJAL
Third Assistant Director	NICOLAS CUBRIA
Production Coordinator	BARBARA FACTOROVICH
Location Manager	ALBERTO HASSE
Assistant Location Manager	JACKIE INGBERG
Production Lawyer	JULIO RAFFO
Production Accountant	FERNANDO WAJS
Assistant Accountant	MARIA ROSA PUGLIESE
Production Assistant	CLAUDIA DOURA
Runners	SEBASTIAN ALOI
	JULIO RAFFO, JNR
	JORGE CORREA
Grip	RUBEN BEJARANO
Chief Electrician	EDUARDO BROMAN
Electricians	HUGO SENLLE
	HORACIO ACEVEDO
Steadicam Operator	GUSTAVO MOSQUERA
Video Assistant	MATIAS RISI
Generator Operator	ALVARO DOLGAY
Art Director	GRACIELA ODERIGO
Set Dresser	MARIANA SOURROUILLE
Assistant Art Director	MERCEDES ALFONSIN
Prop Master	SERGIO GUALCO
Construction Manager	PASCOLI HERMANOS
Prop Assistant	DANIEL MONROY
Sculptor	ADRIANA MAESTRI
Paintings	CARMEN CORNEJO
	FERNANDA ABADIA

Wardrobe Assistant	PAULA TARATUTO
Hairdresser	RICARDO FASSAN
Special Effects Supervisor	TOM CUNDOM
Unit Driver	GUSTAVO OLDAN
Minibus Coordinator	JUAN CARLOS FERNANDEZ
Truck Coordinator	PEDRO PORCU
Motor Home	ENRIQUE BELTZA
Truck driver (Camera)	PEDRO RIOBO
Truck driver (Lighting)	CARLOS VILLATINI
Truck driver (Grip)	ANDRES MEDICI
Truck driver (Props)	GUSTAVO SOUTE
Catering	ROBERTO GUISADO
Security Chief	MARCOS MAFFULLI
Additional choreography	GUSTAVO NAVEIRA
	FABIAN SALAS
	CARLOS COPELLO

LONDON CREW

Second Assistant Director	MEL NORTCLIFFE
Assistant Art Director	LUCINDA STURGIS
Pilates Trainers	ANDREAS REYNEKE
	MARIANNE HOEGL
Alexander Technique Teacher	DIANA DANTES
Runner	NIK UDOVICIC
Unit Driver	ROY HYATT

POST-PRODUCTION CREW

Assistant Editor	JULIE CLEMENCIN
Additional Assistants	MURIEL MOREAU
	SOPHIE REINE
	LUDOVIC BERRIVIN
	RAPHAELE URTIN
Assistant Sound Editor	VINCENT GUILLON
Re-recording Mixer	ROBIN O'DONOGHUE
Assistant Re-recording Mixer	DOMINIC LESTER
Re-recording at	TWICKENHAM FILM STUDIOS
Foley Artist	JEAN-PIERRE LELONG
Assistant Foley Artist	MARIO MELCHIORRI
Foley Mixer	JACQUES THOMAS-GERARD
Foley recorded at	LES DAMES AUGUSTINES

ADR Mixer GILLES MISSIR
ADR Editors PATRICE RAFFI
CORINNE RAFFI
ADR recorded at SONODI
Avid supplied by VIDEO REFERENCE
Protools supplied by AUDIO 24 25

MILONGA TRISTE: Performed by Hugo Diaz. Composed by Piana/Manzi. Published by Editorial Musical. Korn Intersong SAIC and Warner/ Chappell Music Ltd. Courtesy of Musimundo S.A.

LA CUMPARSITA: Performed by Phil Kelsall. Composed by Matos Rodriguez. Published by Casa Ricordi-BMG Recordi S.p.A. Ⓟ Grasmere Music Ltd 1987.

RAWSON: Performed by Juan D'Arienzo. Composed by Arolas. Licensed through SADAIC. Ⓟ RCA-BMG (Argentina)1965.

ZUM: Performed by Osvaldo Pugliese. Composed by Piazzola. Published by Lagos (SADAIC). Ⓟ EMI-Odeón SAIC (Argentina) 1944.

DOYNA: Performed by the Klezmatics. Composed by London. Published by Piranha/Psycho Freylekhs Music. Ⓟ Piranha Records 1994 and Green Linnet Records 1995.

PENSALO BIEN: Performed by D'Arienzo/Echaque. Composed by Visciglio/Lopez. Published by Editorial Musical. Korn Intersong SAIC and Warner/Chappell Music Ltd. Ⓟ El Bandoneon-Barna Record LAB S.L. 1938.

GALLO CIEGO: Performed by Osvaldo Pugliese y su Orquesta Tipica. Composed by Bardi. Published by BMG Ricordi S.p.A. (SADIAC). Ⓟ EMI-Odeón SAIC (Argentina) 1943.

LIBERTANGO: Performed by Astor Piazzolla. Composed by Piazzolla. Published by Edizioni Curci/A. Pagani and Eaton Music Ltd. Ⓟ Carosello C.E.M.E.D. S.r.l. Records and Tapes.

I AM YOU: Original recording by Hugo Diaz. Courtesy of Musimundo S.A. Composed by Piana/Manzi. Lyrics and vocals by Sally Potter. Published by Editorial Musical. Korn Intersong SAIC and Warner/Chappell Music Ltd.

I AM YOU: Performed by Sally Potter and Yo-Yo Ma. Composed by Piana/Manzi. Lyrics by Sally Potter. Published by Editorial Musical. Korn Intersong SAIC and Warner/Chappell Music Ltd. Ⓟ Sony Music Entertainment Inc 1997.

QUEJAS DE BANDONEON: Performed by Anibal Troilo. Composed by Filiberto. Published by Pirovano (SADAIC). (P) EMI-Odeón SAIC (Argentina) 1957.

MI BUENOS AIRES QUERIDO: Performed by Carlos Gardel. Composed by Gardel/Lepera. (P) EMI-Odeón SAIC (Argentina) 1927.

EL FLETE: Performed by Juan d'Arienzo. Composed by Gradito/Greco. Published by Perrotti (SADAIC). (P) RCA-BMG (Argentina) 1965.

AMOR Y CELOS: Performed by Juan D'Arienzo. Composed by Padula/Roldan. Published by Perrotti (SADAIC). (P) RCA-BMG (Argentina) 1965.

MILONGA DE MIS AMORES: Performed by Juan D'Arienzo. Composed by Contursi/Laurenz. Published by Perrotti (SADAIC). (P) RCA-BMG (Argentina) 1967.

LA YUMBA: Performed by Osvaldo Pugliese. Composed by Pugliese. Published by Editorial Musical. Korn Intersong SAIC and Warner/Chappell Music Ltd. (P) EMI-Odeón SAIC (Argentina) 1944.

SOÑAR Y NADA MAS: Performed by Alfredo de Angelis y su Orquesta Tipica. Composed by Canaro/Pelay. Published by Peermusic (UK) Ltd. (P) El Bandoneon-Barna Records LAB S.L. 1944.

BAHIA BLANCA: Performed by Carlos Di Sarli. Composed by Di Sarli. Published by Peermusic (UK) Ltd. (P) RCA-BMG (Argentina) 1967.

Original Music by SALLY POTTER
With the participation of FRED FRITH

Music performed by
THOMAS BLOCH – Ondes Martenot, Cristal Bachet
FRED FRITH – Guitars, Violin
SALLY POTTER – Vocals

Music recorded at STUDIOS MERJITHUR
Recording Mixer FRANK LEBON
Music Supervisor IVAN CHANDLER, MUSICALITIES
Soundtrack available on SONY CLASSICAL

Freight Agent	DYNAMIC INTERNATIONAL
Insurance Services	AON/ALBERT G. RUBEN
Completion Bond	FILM FINANCES SERVICES LTD
Aaton Camera	ICE FILM EQUIPMENT
Lighting Equipment	ARRI BELL LIGHTING
Lighting Equipment, Argentina	CAMERAS & LUCES S.A.

Titles	RANCH ASSOCIATES
	STEVE MASTERS
Optical Effects	PEERLESS CAMERA COMPANY
Film Processing	METROCOLOR LONDON
Laboratory Liaison	CLIVE NOAKES
Grader	BOB RODGER
Negative Cutting	TRU-CUT

Arriflex Camera by ARRI/MEDIA

Film stock supplied by KODAK

DOLBY DIGITAL in selected theatres

With special thanks to:
Jeff Anderson, Kim Ballard, Simon Broad, Reinhard Brundig, Alexandra
Cann, Shaun Coyne, Lindy Davies, Mark Dunford, Jacqueline Dupuy,
Graham Easton, Thomas Esser, Carlos Gavito, Peter Gelb, Ruben
Halperin, Matthijs van Heijningen, Satoru Iseki, Vernon Kemp, Alison
McHale, David Mitchell, Bob Moore, Gustavo Naveira, Kevin O'Shea,
Simon Perry, Caroline Potter, Rabbi Jaime Rosenzweig, Chris Smith,
Kate Wilson

and thanks to:
Instituto Nacional de Cine y Artes Audiovisuales, Argentina
Dirección de Asuntos Consulares,
Ministerio de Relaciones Exteriores, Argentina
Secretaria de Población, Ministerio del Interior, Argentina
Manliba, Departamento de Relaciones para la Comunidad
Templo Israelita, Paso 423, Buenos Aires
Cristalerias San Carlos, Matra Communications, Carlo Manzi,
Grippa y Gaddi, Moulin Galland, Peter Schweiger

This film is supported by the National Lottery
through the Arts Council of England and by Eurimages

A British-French Co-production

Filmed on location in Paris, Buenos Aires and London

Released in the UK by Artificial Eye
Released in the US by Sony Pictures Classics